Ex Libris

C. O. JONES

The C.O. Jones
Compendium of
Practical Jokes

The C. O. Jones Compendium of Practical Jokes

by

Richard Boston

illustrated
by
Posy Simmonds

Enigma Books
L O N D O N

First published 1982 by
Enigma Books
an imprint of Severn House Publishers Limited.
4 Brook Street, London W1Y 1AA

Boston, Richard
    The C.O. Jones compendium of practical jokes

I. Practical jokes
I. Title
    790.1'3   PN6231.P67

ISBN 0 7278 3003 1

Typeset by TJB Photosetting, South Witham,
Lincolnshire
Printed in Great Britain by Hazell Watson & Viney Limited
Aylesbury, Buckinghamshire

Contents

'You young men have too many jokes. When there are no jokes, you have nothing left.'

'Fortunately there are always more jokes,' the ugly young man remarked.

'I don't believe it .. I believe things are getting more serious. You young men will find that out.'

'The increasing seriousness of things .. that is the great opportunity of jokes.'

'They will have to be grim jokes,' said the old man.

Henry James *Portrait of a Lady* 1881

FIRST ENCOUNTERS OF A STRANGE KIND

I'm no good at cricket. I'm also no good at football, golf or snooker. I *would* be good at tennis if the ball went where I want it to slightly more often. I am, however, absolutely brilliant at chess, though for some reason my brilliance is not consistent and tends to fall off at the end of the game. However, I do usually play very well against near-beginners, who are dismayed by the subtlety of my tactics, as explained to them at length in the post mortem.

I used to be pretty good at poker, but it turned out to be too expensive and I had to give it up. I am also no slouch at ping-pong. Unfortunately, most people I meet seem to be even less slouch.

I'm not saying that I'm no good at games. I am good. Very. It's just that I'm no good at the games I've mentioned, or indeed at any of the others I've tried. Why this should be I don't know. It's grossly unfair. I suppose it's a matter of natural aptitude. Some people have a gift for one game, others for others. It's just that I have had the bad luck not to have come across the one I am fitted for. It can only be a matter of time. One day someone will invent a game at which I will be a world-beater. I am confident about this.

Meanwhile, as I wait (patiently), I have to be content to watch other people doing things which I would do so much better than they if only I could get the hang of it. Like playing cricket. Of all the games I am no good at, cricket is easily top. As a batsman I am hopeless, mostly because of my perfectly sensible concern that the ball (which is far too hard and travels at a ridiculous speed) might strike me on my only head. The same goes for fielding in the slips, or anywhere else except on the boundary. The only trouble with the boundary is that it's such a long way from the wicket, and throwing a cricket ball is a knack I never acquired.

I vividly remember my last game of cricket. I was at my usual position of long stop (a placing on the field which seems to have dropped out since my day) and I was rather pleased when a ball, which had got past the wicket-keeper, made its way in my direction reasonably slowly. Having succeeded in stopping it from going over the boundary I picked the thing up and hurled it as hard as I could in the direction of the wicket. The ball soared into the air like a bird. In a surprisingly short time it paused and began its return to earth. When it had completed its almost vertical descent, I realised to my shame that I was still the player on the field who was nearest to the ball. By the time I had run towards it, picked it up and thrown the hateful red object to the wicket, or to a fielder fairly near it, the batsmen had scored five runs. I haven't played cricket since.

So I became a spectator, a role which is not to be sneered at. There's no point in a game which just has players. They also serve who only sit and watch . . . and make caustic comments. And that is what I was doing one summer afternoon some years ago when I first met C.O. Jones.

It was a classic English summer scene. The cawing of rooks in the elms; the crack of leather on willow; the aged villagers fondling their pints and their memories; the visitors with their bored wives and screaming brats (or screaming wives and bored brats); the strawberry tea at the interval; the bitter cold; the warm bitter . . . you've got the picture. At the end of the game (which the home team lost easily) I heaved myself up from the deck-chair and strode in the direction of the pub. I didn't stride very far. At some point in the game I must have dozed off. Some swine had taken advantage of my brief nap to tie the lace of my left shoe to its brother on the right one. Bloody kids, I thought, as I untied the laces and picked myself up. King Herod was greatly misunderstood.

Later on in the pub I sought out the man who had been sitting nearest to me during the match. Perhaps he could throw some light on the identity of the small child who had brought me down. He was a serious-looking chap of medium height, clothed in a way that seemed inappropriate both for the place and the occasion. The thick tweed suit must have been too hot for even an English summer's day. As for the orange and purple bow-tie, the less said the better. Still, he seemed a nice enough sort of person and he listened with a suitable mixture of amusement and sympathy to the story of my downfall. Meanwhile I tried to remember where I had come across him before.

I bought him a drink. He offered me a cigarette. I don't smoke usually, but on this occasion accepted, since I didn't want to interrupt the story I was telling, about Moses coming down from the mountain with the tablets. He calls the Children of Israel and announces the result of his long and tricky negotiations with God. 'First, the good news,' Moses said. 'I got the commandments down to ten. Now the bad news. Adultery is in.'

At the end of the story I picked up a box of matches from the table. When I opened it the contents emptied themselves on the floor. Some damn fool had taken the tray out of the box and replaced it the wrong way up. It was the first time I had consciously realised that the label on a match box is usually on one side only, thereby helpfully informing you which way up to hold it. I had plenty of time to think about this as I retrieved the matches from the floor. By the time I had finished doing so, the man in the orange-and-purple bow-tie had left.

And that was my first meeting with C.O. Jones.

No it wasn't. Some time after he had gone and my temper had returned to normal, I remembered where I had seen him before. 1958, my first trip to Paris. I had done the Eiffel Tower and the Louvre and the Arc de Triomphe. Now for Montmartre, where the pavements were blocked with men in berets standing in front of easels while they pretended to paint ghastly pictures of the Sacré Coeur or picturesque corner cafes with tables outside.

Most of these paintings are in fact knocked off in a sweat-shop in Yugoslavia. All the street 'artist' does is to add a few brush-strokes of blue to the sky so that the punters will think the canvas is freshly painted. There are always plenty of mindless tourists around who relax from the strain of peering through their camera view-finders to gawp at these bogus paintings. They even pay out hard cash for the daubs, doubtless in the fond belief that they have discovered a new Utrillo, or van Gogh, or Modigliani, while simultaneously enjoying the fantasy that they are Gene Kelly or Fred Astaire (or girl friend of one or other, or both).

On that particular day in Montmartre, all those years ago, there was one of these artists who had collected an unusually large crowd about him. The reason was easily discovered. Although he was well placed for a good view of the Sacré Coeur (in so far as there *is* a good view of it) that monstrous pile was not what he was painting. Instead,

4

his canvas depicted, in considerable detail, a very lovely young lady lying on a bed with nothing on apart from an expression that seemed to combine invitation and satisfaction.

I imagine that C.O. Jones (for it was he) would have easily found a buyer. Unfortunately his act did not go down well with his fellow artists. They may have been stupid... indeed, they almost certainly were... but even they could see that he was taking the mickey and that, while he might be raising the intellectual tone of the neighbourhood, he was not going to be good for trade. A few of the bigger ones gathered round and made it clear that his presence was not welcome. In fact he was given *cinq minutes* in which to make himself scarce.

C.O. (I never did discover what the initials stood for) was in those days an art student. There were ulterior motives for this – and I'll reveal more about C.O.'s involvement with the arts later on. I subsequently learned that his Montmartre joke was a variant on one he used in the Life Class of the Regent Street Polytechnic School of Art. He would sit down in front of the model, gaze at her with intense concentration, work busily away and produce a picture of the Sacré Coeur.

A few weeks after the cricket match I bumped into him again in a rather grotty pub in Camden Town. At closing time, since the night seemed young and he hadn't tied my shoelaces together all evening, I suggested that we might continue with a drink or two at my place. By the time we had finished the bottle of whisky (which by good luck he happened to have with him) it was 2.30 in the morning. I still didn't know much about him, since he was vague (even secretive) about many details of his life. It did emerge, however, that he spent a fair bit of time devising and carrying out practical jokes and hoaxes of varying complexity. Usually they were original, but he did not hesitate to pinch ideas from the work of other masters when he felt like it.

His hotel joke was, I believe, original. At any rate he had carried it out only recently. He told me that he had been staying (at the expense of a client... what kind of client?... he didn't want to go into that) in one of those expensive modern hotels where each room is provided with such modern conveniences as colour television, a cocktail cabinet and a Gideon Bible, in addition to the usual things like a towel and stationery bearing the hotel's address.

C.O. happened to remember that a colleague called Dale had been staying at this same hotel a few days earlier. Taking a sheet of the hotel's headed paper he wrote Dale a letter which purported to come from the hotel management. It complained in formal but firm terms about the condition in which the hotel staff (respectable women) had found the sheets on Mr Dale's bed after he left. He demanded eight pounds as a contribution towards the cost of new bed linen.

The extraordinary thing is that Dale paid up. Or so Jones said. How he could have found out, I can't imagine. It's hardly the kind of thing Dale would have gone round boasting about.

The next one he told me was probably cribbed, but it gave C.O. a lot of pleasure. He was working in a large advertising agency at the time. Well, not working exactly. Since the agency wasn't doing too well, and since Jones was at the best of times exceptionally lazy, he used to spend most of his office hours staring out of the window at life's panorama passing by in the street below.

He noticed that this particular street had a bus stop quite close to a public telephone box. These simple ingredients were sufficient for his mischievous brain to work on. First he took the opportunity of the next tea-break to nip down into the street and discover the number of the telephone. Then he returned to his desk and waited for the right combination of events to occur. This did not take long, since all he needed was a reasonably long bus queue and someone wanting to use the telephone. Then he dialled all the numbers of the public telephone except for the last one.

The first person wanting to use the telephone was a man in an anorak. Just as he was opening the door of the call-box, C.O. dialled the last number. The man in the anorak hesitated a moment and then picked up the phone.

Man in anorak: Sorry mate, this is a public call box.

C.O. Jones: Yes, I know it is, but I wonder if you can help me. The thing is that I know that the call-box you're in is next to the bus stop and my wife always takes the bus about this time of day. She's got blonde hair and she's wearing a blue coat . . .

(Jones then described in detail someone in the bus queue.)

C.O. Jones: Can you see her?

Man in anorak: Yes, I can see her. Hang on, guv, I'll go and tell her.

After which, all Jones had to do was sit back and watch the man in the anorak approach a total stranger in a bus queue to inform her that she was wanted on the phone.

C.O. used to spend entire days like that. Doubtless he would still be doing so, had he not been fired. By the time we had finished the whisky, C.O. had told me many such stories, after which I still didn't know much about him though my knowledge of practical jokes was much greater. As it was too late for him to get home (if he ever had a home, which I doubt) I offered him the spare bedroom for the night.

He stayed for nearly four years, calmly surviving the many domestic, marital and amatory upheavals that went on around him. Of these there were plenty, since during that period I shared the flat with a variety of people. There were plenty of rooms, and the turnover of population was steady. Not everyone paid a fair share of the rent every month, but somehow we muddled through, which is surprising considering that there were some pretty odd characters. There was a solicitor with a taste for lorry drivers, and an air hostess with a taste for lorry-drivers, and a lorry-driver with a taste for ... but that's another story.

C.O. was impervious to these comings and goings, except in so far as he contributed to them. He was equally impervious to hints that he might one day (soon) be among the goings. In the end the girl I was with at the time said (well, screamed) that if he didn't go then she would. It wasn't that she didn't like him. She did. She just couldn't stand any more of the pencils which turned out to be made of rubber when she was taking a message on the phone, or the tea-spoon which suddenly bent in half just as she was putting sugar in her tea. Or the left-handed corkscrew. Or the imitation spilt ink. The final straw was the 'Fido's Mistake' which she nearly trod on in the bathroom. C.O. had to go.

He took it surprisingly well, as he did the £200 I lent him to tide him over while he settled somewhere else. I never expected to see the money back, especially when he rang me up the next day to say he had put the lot on a horse that was running at 33-1 in the 2.30 at Newbury on Saturday.

Amazingly, it won. Even more amazingly he sent me £50 a few days later. That was the last I heard of him, except that I still sometimes open a letter and find a couple of fivers in it: I assume they come from him. Last Christmas I received a parcel which gave me a big surprise – and not just because when I opened it a Jack-in-the-Box jumped out. That was indeed surprising, though not so much as the fact that it was accompanied by no fewer than four fivers. C.O. is not a bad chap at heart. He just suffers from diminished responsibility.

Since I reckon he still owes me about a hundred quid (plus interest over several years), I have not hesitated in this book to make use of the notes and newspaper cuttings about practical jokes which I found in the several cardboard boxes he left behind in his room. The same goes for the press cuttings that occasionally reach me by mail without any covering letter. (How many are reports of his own work I have no idea).

C.O. delighted not only in thinking up and perpetrating hoaxes, but also in narrating past exploits of his own and of other like-minded people, alive and dead. He had also given some thought to the theoretical aspects of the business, including the psychological factors which cause certain individuals (almost invariably male) to go in for this kind of foolish behaviour. I didn't always agree with him, but freely acknowledge the debt I owe him in the way of ideas and information about the theory and practice of practical jokes that he would pour out from time to time, usually when television had closed down for the night and he didn't feel like going to bed.

I think it's only fair for me to draw on his researches and inventions in this way. Apart from the money, it will be compensation for the large bunch of flowers that arrived shortly after a trip to Edinburgh that I made on my own not long ago. The flowers were very nice. What didn't go down so well domestically was the accompanying card reading, 'Darling, I will never forget those nights. xxx Maggie'. *That* took some explaining, I can tell you. Anyway, how did he know I'd been to Edinburgh? I'm not the only one who would like an answer to that question. And no, I don't know anyone called Maggie, in Edinburgh or anywhere else.

9

It is sometimes said that there is only one basic practical joke, which is the stout gentleman slipping on the banana skin. This is nearly true, but not quite. If the banana skin is one that merely happens to be lying on the High Street pavement, and the stout gentleman is some anonymous person who has just got off the bus, the result of the frictionless contact between his shoe, the skin of the banana and the surface of the pavement is an accident, and all good men will come to the aid of the stout party.

If, on the other hand, the portly gentleman is the detested geography teacher who has been tyrannising the fourth form throughout the term, and if the banana skin has been strategically placed by Robinson Jr with malice aforethought, then the result is laughter unconfined. The same goes for the drawing-pin on the chair.

C.O. Jones always stressed the importance of distinguishing between the accidental and the deliberately contrived, and between the malicious and the ingeniously comic. To shout 'Fire' in a crowded stadium may be a hoax, but there's nothing funny about it. Likewise to wire up a car so that it explodes when someone gets into it is murder, whereas to conceal a farting cushion on the driving seat can, in the right circumstances, be very funny.

The *Shorter Oxford Dictionary* says that a practical joke is 'a trick played on some person usually to have a laugh at his expense'. For a practical joke to cause embarrassment and confusion is one thing. To cause actual bodily harm, on the other hand, is not a laughing matter.

This distinction is now enshrined in law. Perhaps it always has been. At any rate on 4 July 1980, *The Times* reported a debate in the House of Lords under the heading 'Peers Agree to Create Only a Little Stink'. Discussing the Novelties (Safety) Regulations, Lord Trefarne, a Lord in Waiting, said that the traditional stink bomb, contained in glass capsules designed to be broken underfoot, would not be banned by the Regulations, which were designed only to prohibit large stink bombs. Large stink bombs, he explained (showing a knowledge of the subject highly creditable in a Lord in Waiting), were sold in plastic bottles with a screw cap, thereby enabling hooligans to throw the contents in people's eyes. Therefore the Regulations would ban stink bombs containing more than 1.5 ml of liquid consisting of sulphides of ammonia, or a mixture or solution of such sulphides.

Lord Trefarne's command of his subject won the applause of his peers. He explained that the products known in the trade as novelties were 'inexpensive products for pastimes or jokes, sometimes designed to create amusement at the expense of unsuspecting victims'. (Cheers) Similar products, he continued, included sneezing powders, fake lumps of sugar, food made from plastic, glasses that emptied their contents, and blood-stained bandages. (Renewed cheers). None of these was likely to cause personal injury.

The dictionary and the House of Lords rightly distinguish between what causes the victim(s) to be embarrassed and look foolish and what might cause him, her or them to suffer personal, physical, financial and any other real injury.

Some of the most hilarious comedies ever written have revolved around ingenious practical jokes. One thinks of the tricks that Prince Hal played on Falstaff; of Sir Toby Belch's ruse to convince the wretched Malvolio that the countess Olivia had fallen in love with him; of Goldsmith's *She Stoops to Conquer* in which the rich young man is duped by Tony Lumpkin into believing that he is staying at an inn when in fact he is in the house of his prospective parents-in-law (whom naturally he treats as though they are the inn-keeper and his wife, haughtily ordering food and wine, complaining about his room and so on).

Much as C.O. enjoyed the hoaxes of fiction and drama he was far more interested in those which have actually been perpetrated in what he called 'real life'. Consequently the aim of this book (which is his as much as it is mine) is not to investigate the bizarre mentality of the practical joker, or to make yet another hopeless attempt to define the sources or mechanisms of wit, humour or jokes. If that's what you're after, then you would do better to consult the works on the subject by the late Professors Bergson and Freud, or even my own modest tome *An Anatomy of Laughter*(Collins, 1974) which paddles in the shallower regions of those murky waters. In the present book, by contrast, the jokes are not intended to be used as specimens for analysis or to illustrate any particular theory. They are here in their own right, intended for entertainment rather than instruction.

I cannot end this preamble without a brief warning of the kind printed on cigarette packets. Practical jokes are by their nature irresponsible, but there are limits. Jokes are not funny if they cause harm — financial, physical, psychological or anything-else-ological. For this reason frauds and forgeries do not come into the category of hoaxes and practical jokes. Anyone wishing to repeat or emulate any of the hoaxes described in this book should also bear in mind that wasting police time is a serious offence, and that bogus calls to ambulances and fire brigades can cost lives. Such japes are malicious and not funny. Here endeth the lesson.

It only remains for me to thank all those friends and acquaintances who have suggested material for this book, and to acknowledge the particular debts I owe to my publisher David Harsent, and to my bank manager. And of course to Posy Simmonds who drew the pictures.

HORS D'OEUVRES VARIEES
OR ANTIPASTO MISTO

The picture desk of a national newspaper is a busy place and usually a friendly one. It has to be busy because there is often very little time in which to come up with the right picture for the right story. At the same time the staff have to deal with all sorts of people from editors and writers to photographers who have just returned from snapping Fidel Castro, Prince Charles, Alexander Solzhenitsyn, Anna Ford, Johnny Rotten or whoever else may currently be in the public eye. It's usually a hectic place, but a cheerful one.

It was to such a place that one day a man called Potts came to work. *Mr* Potts, to be precise (which he certainly was). He made it clear that first names were not for him and that in general he considered himself to be a cut above the rest of his colleagues. Naturally the lads construed this as an invitation to take him down a peg or two.

It so happened that Mr Potts was in the habit of wearing a particularly objectionable green pork-pie hat. When he arrived every morning at precisely ten o'clock he would say 'Good morning', twitch his tooth-brush moustache, put the hat on a peg and proceed to his desk. When he left in the afternoon he would reverse the process, twitching his moustache, placing hat on head, turning to his colleagues, saying 'Good afternoon' and leaving.

What they did was this. One day when he was out of the

room they examined the hat very carefully. Then one of them went round all the hat-shops in the area until he managed to find a green pork-pie hat which was identical to Mr Potts'. Identical except that it was quite a bit larger. He bought this, returned to the office and swapped the hats.

At the end of the afternoon Mr Potts followed his normal routine, except that when he put the hat on his head it dropped down over his eyes. This rather spoiled his exit, which was naturally followed by general hilarity.

The next day, to everyone's surprise, Mr Potts turned up with the hat in its normal position. They were puzzled as to how he had achieved this, and at the first opportunity inspected the hat. It turned out that what he had done was to take some strips of newspaper and pad them round the inside of the brim, thereby reducing its diameter.

So what they did next was to take the *original* hat, pad the inside with strips of newspaper, and then again swap hats. At the end of the day when Mr Potts said 'Good afternoon' and put his hat on his head, it merely perched precariously on the very top.

They kept on switching hats in this way for some days. In the end (according to C.O. Jones) Mr Potts went to his doctor, complaining that his head kept getting bigger and smaller. The doctor said there was no such complaint.

Some years ago John Arlott, the writer and broadcaster on wine, cricket and other enjoyable subjects, was proceeding in a westerly direction on a visit to Kingsley Amis, who was then teaching at a university in Wales. Stopping for petrol on the way, Arlott's son Jimmy (an accomplished mimic) took the opportunity to phone the author of *Lucky Jim*. Speaking in a Peter Sellers Indian accent he announced that he was Professor Chatterjee, that he was a great admirer of Amis's work, that he was in the neighbourhood and could he visit Mr Amis that afternoon in order to discuss the state of modern literature?

Amis refused politely, but firmly. He regretted that he already had an engagement and at such short notice would not be able to fit Professor Chatterjee in. The pseudo-Indian was upset by this. 'I have come all the way from Calcutta to discuss modern literature with you, and you will not see me.'

Amis: I'm terribly sorry, old chap, but it's just not possible today.

Chatterjee: It is because I am *black* that you will not see me.

Amis: That's got nothing to do with it at all. It wouldn't make any difference if you were blue or pink or all the colours of the rainbow. I've got some cricket commentator chap coming to see me this afternoon. I'm going to be busy all day. That's all there is to it. I'm very sorry.

Finally the Indian accepted defeat. He could not see Mr Amis, but – 'Excuse me, Mr Amis, may I stand outside and look at your house?'

When the Arlotts arrived, Amis ushered them in quickly. 'Come in, for God's sake,' he said. 'There's an Indian professor outside who I don't want to see me.'

It took some time to convince Amis (himself a noted mimic) that there was no Indian – only young Arlott. Once in on the joke Amis was so delighted that he thought it worth repeating. Accordingly Jimmy Arlott rang up the head of Amis's university department, again announcing that he was Professor Chatterjee from Calcutta, that he was in the neighbourhood and would like to come and discuss Dryden's *Absalom and Achitophel* with him.

This happened during the University vacation, and the Professor was evidently enjoying his leisure. He regretted that a meeting to discuss *Absalom and Achitophel* was not possible that day.

'But it is most important,' said Chatterjee. 'I have noticed that *Absalom and Achitophel* has many interesting resemblances to certain Hindu poems.'

'Oh yes,' said the Professor, 'everyone knows that.' Then the Professor came up with a bright idea. 'The man you want to talk to is a young lecturer of ours called Amis. He knows everything about *Absalom and Achitophel*. I'll give you his number.'

At the beginning of the next term the Professor said to Amis, 'I hope you didn't mind my putting that Indian on to you.' 'Not at all,' Amis replied. 'He turned out to be a very nice chap. He brought me a dozen bottles of champagne.'

A.G.Macdonell carved his small niche in the halls of fame with *England, Their England*, the book that contains the classic, and much anthologised account of the village cricket match. The rest of the book is largely forgotten, but it does contain other good things, most of which (like the cricket match) are closely based on fact.

One of these is the episode in which Macdonell (Donald in the novel) is about to spend a weekend at a grand country house. The young Scotsman is inexperienced in the niceties of upper-class English life, and his friend Huggins warns him of the perils he may encounter. Chief among these is the contempt of the butler and the giggles of the footman which will be incurred if he fails to convince them of his social importance and distinction.

Huggins insists that the best way of impressing domestic staff is by the quantity of luggage that accompanies his arrival. Huggins therefore helpfully buys Donald a number of second-hand suitcases, fills them with rubbish, and pastes them with labels reading 'Beagling Kit', 'Amateur Theatricals', 'Despatches: Secret', and so on. Encumbered with these Donald sets off for the country, being seen off at the station by the assiduous Huggins, whose parting words are a promise to 'fix that bloody butler'.

This he does by a succession of telephone calls in various assumed voices. As a result Donald is greeted on his arrival by an extremely deferential butler who informs him in a confidential tone that 'The Secretary of the French Foreign Ministry rang up, sir, and Budapest has also been on the line. Budapest is to telephone again, sir.'

As for Donald's hostess, she greets him with the information that 'The Duke of Devonshire has been on the telephone. You are on no account to telephone him, but you are to go to Chatsworth in time for luncheon on Monday, and to say nothing to anyone.' According to Richard Ingrams's introduction to his collection of the works of Beachcomber (J.B. Morton) this is an accurate account of a real event, Huggins being J.B. Morton, and the hostess Lady Houston, a wealthy lady whose notable contribution to the suffragette movement consisted of training 615 parrots to screech 'Votes for Women'.

One of Morton's most bizarre – almost surrealist – practical jokes was perpetrated in Guildford (a town which C.O. always felt could benefit from a little brightening up). Morton was walking down the main street when he stopped at a pillar box and started talking into the slot you put the letters in. He pretended that a small boy had somehow trapped himself inside. 'Are you all right, my little man?' he asked. 'Don't worry, we'll soon get you out.' When a curious crowd had assembled and the fire brigade had been summoned, Morton quietly slipped away leaving a number of puzzled Guildfordians making reassuring noises to the pillar box.

Morton was once on a train that stopped at Harrow station. Seeing a group of schoolboys on the platform, he leant out of the window and announced, 'Boys! I am Dr Smallcroft, your new headmaster.' He then turned back into the compartment and commanded in a falsetto voice, 'Put the horses in the other end of the train,' to which he replied in his normal voice, 'No, my dear, they'll be perfectly all right here.'

Practical jokes thrive particularly well in places where young people find themselves living away from home for the first time. Free from the restraints of family, school and other institutions of society which attempt to make them behave sensibly, their fancy lightly turns to thoughts of pranks.

Student halls of residence, colleges and boarding-houses are therefore particularly fertile breeding-grounds, and when the perpetrators are bright as well as mischievous their tricks can reach levels of ingenuity considerably higher than the schoolboy's drawing-pin on the teacher's chair, or the bucket of water over the door.

C.O. once shared a flat with a group of students, one of whom, Raine, was exceptionally particular about the way his eggs were boiled. The white had to be firm, but the yolk just runny. This required very precise timing.

It was a simple business for C.O. to hard-boil the eggs beforehand and leave them in the fridge. Day after day Raine found his breakfast egg cooked solid right through. Day after day he reduced the cooking-time. When he was down to about half a minute's boiling-time, C.O. let him have uncooked eggs, which naturally spilt all over the plate.

Raine was not stupid, though. Having twigged what was happening, he worked out a way to tell the difference between a boiled egg and an unboiled one without cracking it. I now pass on this information (which is surely in itself worth the price of this book) to all who live in fear of falling victim to practical jokers. What you do is take the egg and place it on its side on a table. Spin it (the egg, not the table, you fool). If it spins regularly on its axis, then it is hard-boiled. If it wobbles eccentrically, it is because the yolk is swishing about inside, and therefore the egg is uncooked. However, most cooks are not on their guard against foolish behaviour of this kind and if you know that a cake or an omelette is to be made later in the day, then a few minutes can always be usefully spent in hard-boiling an egg and replacing it in its cardboard receptacle along with its untreated fellows. Pour yourself a drink and watch the cook at work as he or she cracks the eggs into a bowl. Watch, and enjoy, the expression on the cook's face when the hard-boiled egg is taken out and attempt after attempt to break the egg on the side of the bowl fails to do

more than crack the shell.

Eggs provide enormous opportunities for the practical joker. For example, you can blow them, as egg-collectors used to do. Having chipped a tiny hole at one end, it is possible with patience and a thin knitting needle to extract all the contents. Place the empty shell among the other eggs in the box, and again observe the expressions of considerable confusion which may be observed on the face of the cook.

Joke shops sell quite realistic fried eggs – though in my view the yolks are usually rather small. But verisimilitude can be added by serving them with bacon and fried tomatoes at breakfast time. Pour the bacon fat over the egg and it is indistinguishable from the real thing – at least to the unsuspecting, who may saw away with the knife for some time before protesting at the toughness of the egg.

This trick worked successfully on my friend Jacques Seysses on a recent visit to England. Jacques is a Burgundy *vigneron* who produces about the best wine I've ever tasted. A bottle of his Clos Saint-Denis, Domaine Dujac, 1973, was among my most treasured possessions until one day when my will-power was weak and the off-licence was closed. Now I have only the memory to treasure.

On a return visit to the home of Jacques and his charming wife, I did not fail to arrive at Moray-St Denis well-armed with such joke-shop products as a plastic kipper, plastic bacon, plastic fried egg, false ears, foaming blood capsules, spectacles with attached false nose and moustache, and other gifts. These were gratefully received.

Jacques decided to try out the fried egg first. He chose as victim one of his grape-pickers, an intrepid and lovely New Zealander called Ann, who had offended him by repeatedly beating him at badminton.

Meals in the Seysses household are of wonderful and delicious gastronomic complexity, but on this particular evening Jacques announced that we would be simply having fried eggs – a suggestion that was welcome after the stomach-straining generosity of the meals of previous days. All but Ann were drawn into the conspiracy by which she would receive the plastic egg.

This provided an opportunity to twist the joke round, so that Jacques should be the victim. First Ann was informed as to what was going on. Next, we took a real egg and fried it very slowly until it was solid right through. Then we carefully removed the fake egg from its plastic envelope, substituted the real one and re-stapled the envelope.

Jacques took over the cooking, with suppressed giggling in the background – giggling which he naturally assumed was in anticipation of Ann's imminent fate. It only needed

a small diversion – 'Ann, would you mind fetching another glass' – for him to take out what he supposed was a plastic egg from its transparent packet and slip it onto her plate. On her return we sat down to the meal. To Jacques' visible astonishment, Ann ate the egg.

He got his revenge though. On the day we were leaving he revealed that the soap in the bathroom we had been using was also plastic in material and joke-shop in origin. The fact that we had not noticed was taken as a hilarious comment on our standards of personal hygiene. For myself, I couldn't see anything funny about this at all.

These egg tricks have caused me to digress from the subject of student jokes. Here's one C.O. rather liked. In Winchester there's a square dominated by a very large statue of King Alfred the Great. A less impressive feature of the place is the Public Convenience. One dark night some students painted footsteps from the feet of the statue of King Alfred, down the steps to the Gents and back again to his place on the plinth. After all those years the poor chap must have needed some relief.

Until very recently the colleges of Oxford and Cambridge enforced extremely strict rules about the time by which undergraduates had to be back inside at night. Those returning after the curfew hour without prior permission either had to pay a fine or else enter illegally, evading the patrolling porters by climbing over dangerously spiked walls. To prevent entry through windows facing onto the street there were iron bars which were placed too closely together for a human body to pass through.

It was, C.O. Jones claims, at Gonville and Caius College, Cambridge, that the following trick was played. A ground-floor room, with grilled window, facing onto Trinity Street, a fairly busy thoroughfare of that university city, was occupied by an elderly Professor of some obscure subject. In the room immediately above him dwelt a mischievous young man who, in the middle of a busy weekday, while bored with his studies and having nothing better to do, found himself staring at his chamber pot. (The ancient colleges of Cambridge, with their mediaeval plumbing and heating systems, made chamber pots, in those days possessions as essential as hot-water bottles.)

The young man tied a long piece of string to the handle of the china chamber pot, which he then lowered from his own window to the grilled window of the Professor of some obscure subject below him. His repeated knocking of the pot against the window first attracted the Professor's attention and then succeeded in irritating him. In exasperation he opened the window and seized the chamber pot, whereupon the student above let go of the string. The Professor tried to take the pot in, but his arm was between the bars of the window, which were too closely spaced to allow the passage of the chamber pot. He was reluctant to let go, because the pot would drop onto the pavement outside and shatter. He was therefore stuck with his hand out of the window holding a potty out onto the thorough-fare. Passers-by assumed that he was collecting for charity

and started dropping small coins into the pot, which became increasingly difficult to release as the collection grew. An embarrassing predicament for an elderly academic to find himself in. C.O. rated this one 8 out of 10.

Touring actors, musicians and other performers are familiar with the hazards of boarding-houses and their often dragonish proprieters. Arthur Askey tells a story of a comedian colleague of his who found himself staying in such an establishment. Foreseeing the unpleasant eventuality of finding himself on dry premises outside licensing hours he bought a bottle of sherry, which he placed in a cupboard. When he came to avail himself of the sherry he found that the bottle had been opened and the level reduced by a couple of inches. Clearly the work of the landlady. If she was going to pinch his booze, there was only one thing to do – unbutton his flies and top the bottle up.

The same thing happened several days running. When the comedian was leaving and paying his bill, the landlady said she looked forward to his staying again. 'Not on your life', he said, and made it quite clear that he was fully aware of the way his sherry had been daily appropriated. The landlady's reply was devastating. She said she knew how much he liked sherry in his trifle and had been adding it as an ingredient throughout the week's meals. C.O. would quote this story as what he called a Boomerang.

On the Parkinson show Michael York described staying with Oliver Reed at some huge hotel where the reception area was dominated by a large pond populated with goldfish and water-lilies. Reed got some carrots, cut them lengthways into shapes like goldfish. Then he went to the pond, put his hand in the water, pulled out what was apparently a goldfish, popped it into his mouth and munched it up. The management asked him to leave the hotel.

Actually the carrot as goldfish is quite an old music-hall gag. C.O. knew of one comedian who used the illusion regularly, but cut it from his act after a colleague seasoned the carrot generously with cayenne pepper.

The illusion of the carrot-fish, the business of deception as part of the practical joke, particularly intrigued C.O. He would recount, with obvious pleasure, a practical joke which involved what he believed to be one of the most brilliant deceptions: brilliant because the joker used the power of the victim's imagination in order to create the illusion. The story, in C.O.'s rendition, is attributed to Barry Humphries (or Dame Edna Everage, or both) and involved a sustained effort, topped by a superb pay-off.

One morning, Humphries went into a neighbourhood chemist's shop and asked for a box of soap – some well-known brand. It was given to him, he paid, then started to leave the shop without taking the soap with him.

'You've forgotten your soap, sir,' called the chemist. Humphries walked back to the counter. 'I don't want the soap,' he said. 'All I want is the experience of buying it from you. It's important to me.' Then he left, while the bemused chemist restored the bar of soap to the pile on the shelf.

Every morning for a month, Humphries performed the same act. He'd walk into the chemist's, ask for a certain brand of soap, pay for it and leave without it, each time claiming that he wanted not the soap, but the human contact involved – the existential experience of purchasing it. By this time the chemist had become quite accustomed to taking fifty pence or whatever from this amiable loony each morning. Then came the moment for the joke to be sprung.

On the thirtieth or so day, Humphries entered the chemist's and made his usual request. The chemist put the soap on the counter and went to the till with Humphries's money. This time, however, Humphries took the soap, put it in his coat pocket and brought out another bar, wrapped in just the same way and to all intents and purposes

25

exactly identical, which he switched with the first bar, making a rather clumsy and obvious job of doing so. He then went through the 'I just want the *experience* of buying it from you' routine and left. Sitting on the counter was the substituted bar of soap.

The chemist probably scratched his head a bit and pondered the matter ... each day a man comes in and asks for soap, pays for it, then leaves it behind – or *appears* to leave it behind. At this point, the chemist might have been afflicted by tiny doubts. He would have unwrapped the bar of soap. And he would have found, neatly re-wrapped inside, a block of cooking lard. Again, perhaps, it might have taken a moment or two before the awful possibility dawned and he turned to the pile of soap on the shelf behind him. *Every morning for a month!* C.O. often used to speculate about how many bars the chemist would have had to unwrap before he realised that the lard had been substituted on just the one occasion.

Douglas Fairbanks, too, was a practical joker, and he had the financial resources to perform fairly elaborate japes. For example he had a chair made that gave a mild electric shock to anyone sitting in it. On one occasion a visiting young lady sat in the chair and didn't react. Fairbanks was puzzled, and asked if she hadn't felt anything. Yes, she replied, but she had simply thought that it was what you *would* feel on first sitting down with a glamorous star like Fairbanks. Not quite one of C.O.'s 'boomerangs' perhaps –

more a total flop. C.O. lived in mortal fear of flops.

It was a small Australian town the name of which Clive James would doubtless know but which I have forgotten. C.O. did tell me but I'm not at all sure that he wasn't relying more heavily on invention than on recollection. I think he said it was Wagga-Wagga, or Bugga-Bugga ... something like that. Anyway, it was a small town in that large country – probably undistinguished by anything but the fact that it was the location for what C.O. referred to as 'a perfect example of the practical joke *in absentia*'.

To begin with, posters began to appear in public places announcing, in very large type: HE IS COMING! After a few days these were replaced by posters which said in even bolder type: HE IS COMING SOON!!! Puzzled interest began to mount among the entertainment-starved population of Bugga-Jagga, and speculation was of the rife variety as they sank their cold tubes of Foster's of an evening, and a morning and an afternoon – and a night. There was wonder in Chunderland.

Then came the poster: HE IS COMING ON THURSDAY, followed by details of the time, the hall and the admission price. On the appointed day the place was packed. The appointed hour arrived too, but the curtains on the stage didn't stir. Australians are very good at things like diving and tennis, and they're not all that bad at cricket, but they are not famous for their patience or for any reluctance to express their feelings. Vocal protest crescendoed, expressed in that Australian version of the language of Chaucer, Shakespeare and Milton which can turn the air snot-green and make the paint peel off the wall.

Finally the curtains opened, only to reveal a notice saying: HE HAS GONE. Which he had. With the takings.

You won't find Bugga-Jagga on the map. Doubtless it was wiped out in the aftermath.

BY HOOK OR BY CROOK

Why is it that the greatest practical jokers often have names beginning with 'H'? There's no answer to that, as Eric Morcambe would say. The fact is, though, that there are (as far as I know) only three people who are remembered solely as practical jokers, and their names are Hugh Troy, Horace de Vere Cole and Theodore Hook.

Theodore Edward Hook (1788-1841), playwright, novelist and musical composer, early developed a keen sense of mischief. He particularly enjoyed disrupting theatrical performances. During a Drury Lane tragedy he hid under the stage and accompanied the leading man's big speech by playing on a penny whistle. On another occasion he interrupted a play by rushing on stage with a letter which he thrust into the hands of the leading actor, informing him that he had come into a fortune.

These japes were small fry compared with the Berners Street hoax, one of the most elaborate practical jokes ever played. It happened in 1809 and centred on 54 Berners Street. According to some accounts Hook made a bet that within eight days he could make this plain address the most famous in London. Other versions have it that Hook had a score to settle with the lady who lived at that address, a Mrs Tottenham.

In any case, what Hook did was to write an enormous number of letters – more than 4,000 of them. As a result of these, on a particular day there arrived at 54 Berners Street an armada of vehicles, some delivering coal, some furniture, one other a wedding cake. There were hearses and hay-carts; there were chimney-sweepers, butchers, bakers, candlestick makers, lawyers, doctors, dentists, fishmongers and every other conceivable kind of tradesman. The confusion was completed by the arrival of the Duke of Gloucester, the Lord Mayor of London and a host of other dignitaries lured to Berners Street on some pretext or other in one of Hook's letters. Hook, who had rented a room on the opposite side of the street, was able to sit by the window and enjoy the spectacle.

The Prince Regent was amused by the affair and rewarded Hook with a cushy job as Accountant-General and Treasurer at Mauritius. The salary was £2,000 a year – a pretty penny in those days – and the work involved was minimal. Even so Hook found himself unable to manage even the smallest effort, and through idleness and incompetence managed to mislay £62,000, landing himself in jug for two years as a result.

Later he had a distinguished, if disreputable, journalistic career as editor of the scurrilous satirical *John Bull*, the *Private Eye* of its day, and he was immortalised as Mr Wagg in Thackeray's *Vanity Fair*. The *Dictionary of National Biography* says that Hook was 'wanting in every quality especially characteristic of a high-minded man'. C.O. Jones was not too pleased when I pointed out to him that it is this very imperfection of character that is such a vital ingredient in the psychological make-up of a compulsive practical joker such as Hook (and C.O.) undoubtedly were.

Whether the Berners Street hoax could be repeated today is extremely unlikely, since tradesman nowadays never turn up on the appointed day, let alone at the appointed time.

Among the great practical jokers whose work C.O. Jones had studied and emulated, he put the American Hugh Troy among the top three or four. C.O.'s voluminous files do not reveal Troy's dates: the only indication is that, as we shall see, he served in the United States army during the Second World War. What C.O. particularly admired about Troy was the economy, the ingenuity and the lack of malice that were the hallmarks of a Troy prank.

Like many adolescents, Troy wrote poems, an enterprise in which he was not encouraged by his sister who made the kind of disparaging remarks about his literary efforts that only sisters can. 'Why bother to write them?' she asked. 'They'll never be published.'

Troy replied by betting that he could get one of his poems published within a month.

First he wrote a letter to the literary editor of the *New York Times*. It read as follows:

Dear Sirs,

I am anxious to find a piece of poetry by an American, I believe, with some particularly moving stanzas about a gypsy maiden abandoned on the trail by her tribe.

(signed) Titus Grisby, New York.

This letter was published by the *New York Times*. Troy then followed up with another letter, which read as follows:

Dear Sir,

Titus Grisby must be referring to the beautiful 'Curse of the Gypsy' written in 1870 by the celebrated Poet Laureate of Syracuse, New York, Hugh Troy.

(signed) G. Claude Fletcher, Ithaca, New York.

This was also published, as were the lines of Troy's verse with which he accompanied it.

So we leave her,
So we leave her,
Far from where her swarthy
kindred roam

In the scarlet fever
In the scarlet fever
In the scarlet fever convalescent home.

Troy was a painter and put his skills to good use in the service of practical jokes. As a student at Cornell University he played a trick on a notoriously absent-minded Professor. Appropriating a pair of boots belonging to the learned gentleman, he painted them in such a way that they had the appearance of human feet. When the paint was dry he covered the boots with a water-soluble black substance and returned them to their rightful owner. The next time they were worn on a rainy day, the black was washed off and the oblivious professor walked about the university campus in apparently bare feet.

In 1935 there was a major van Gogh exhibition at the New York Museum of Modern Art which drew such crowds that Troy found it impossible to get a proper view of the paintings. Accordingly, he made a false ear out of wax, returned to the museum on a later occasion with the ear in a tasteful velvet-lined box, and deposited it in a conspicuous place in the gallery accompanied with a printed notice announcing, 'This is the ear which Vincent van Gogh cut off to send his mistress, a French prostitute, on 24 December 1888.' The crowds soon massed around this exhibit, thereby liberating van Gogh's paintings for Troy's unimpeded contemplation.

In C.O.'s files, van Gogh's ear was cross-referenced to another gratuitous donation, as recollected by the architectural historian J.M. Richards. Speaking of the kind of prank that the young John Betjeman used to get up to, he remembers 'his boasting to me one day that he had just come back from the Geological Museum, then housed in a dusty, unvisited red-brick building in Piccadilly by Pennethorne, and had contributed an exhibit of his own. "Do go and look," he said.'

It must have been worth looking at, for Betjeman had found that one of the show cases had been left unlocked. Inside he had placed a small brown object with a neatly lettered card reading 'Horse Chestnut picked up in Bushey Park. Donated by J. Betjeman Esquire'. Apparently it remained there unnoticed, undetected and undisturbed until the building was demolished in 1935 to be replaced by Simpson's store.

Betjeman later received a knighthood for his services to literature. So far his generous contribution to the national collection has gone unhonoured.

But back to Troy, and another museum hoax. One night he deposited outside the Metropolitan Museum of Art, New York, a quantity of burglary equipment – jemmies, wire-cutters, ropes, ladders and so on – along with a number of empty picture-frames. The next day the Director and officials of the museum spent some panic-stricken hours frantically trying to discover which of their master-pieces were missing.

In another assault on the world of art, Troy placed in the *Washington Post* an advertisement: 'Too busy to paint?' it asked. 'We can help you. We paint – you sign.' Styles offered ranged from Impressionist, Cubist and Abstract to Primitive (School of Grandma Moses).

He received a great many enquiries before the hoax was exposed. But this one proved to be another Boomerang. Within a short time similar advertisements were appearing regularly in the American press, but now they were genuine. Evidently Troy had hit on a commercially viable idea. This does happen to humourists, who often find it hard to think up things more fantastic than reality. Beachcomber, for example, invented the electric toothbrush as a joke. He lived to see it as a reality.

It's surprising that none of Troy's hoaxes seem to have got him into serious trouble, especially considering that he did not draw the line at wasting the time of the police.

Troy once bought a green wooden bench of the kind found in public parks. Early one morning, with the help of a friend, he took the bench to Central Park, New York. They placed it in a prominent position and sat down. On the appearance of a patrolling policeman they each took one end of the bench and started carrying it away. 'Hey Mac', said the policeman (or whatever it is that American policemen say). 'Just where the hell do you think you're going with that bench?'

'Home,' said Troy.

'Yeah? You're coming with me to the station.'

Without saying a word, Troy and his friend (still carrying the bench) accompanied the cop to the police station where, on being charged, Troy produced the receipt for the bench.

When Troy was serving in the US Army during the Second World War he soon became fed up with the amount of form-filling involved in fighting Hitler. He thus turned his annoyance into an opportunity. He had some forms printed, requiring information on the subject of Fly papers, Use of. Commanding Officers had to send the Pentagon daily details of how many fly-papers were used in their barracks, precisely where each was placed, how many flies were caught by each paper each day – and so on.

Troy distributed these forms via the usual channels, and was gratified some time later to meet some officers who were in a tizzy because they had received an official rebuke from the Pentagon demanding why they hadn't sent in their fly paper reports. 'Have you heard of fly paper reports?' they asked. 'Of course,' Troy replied. 'I send one in every day.'

Once the military machine begins to move, it is hard to stop. According to Jones there were US Army Officers long after the war who were still sending in daily reports on the kill-rate of their fly papers – doubtless to the deep puzzlement of the KGB.

When Troy was at university, he noticed a friend had a waste-paper basket made out of the foot of a rhinoceros. He waited until a snowy winter's day. Then, with the help of a friend, he filled the rhinoceros foot with heavy weights and attached long ropes to either side. By night the two of them walked through the university, each holding one end of the rope at a considerable distance, lifting and lowering it onto the snow at regular intervals.

The next day the footprints were inspected with great interest, and identified by a zoologist as belonging to a rhino. The footprints led to a lake, where they marched across the ice, ending abruptly at a large hole.

There is something about Venice that invites jokes. For one thing there's so much water for victims to fall into. I think it was Robert Benchley who, on arriving there, sent a cable to a friend in the United States reading: STREETS FLOODED PLEASE ADVISE. And it was of that same beautiful city that the French humorist Alphonse Allais wrote 'The most striking thing about the city of Venice is the complete absence of horse dung.'

He had counted without one of the century's greatest practical jokers. Horace de Vere Cole's honeymoon in 1919 was spent in Venice. The couple's first night together happened to be 1 April. Cole did not spend it in the normal honeymoon manner. Instead he used the cover of darkness to spread quantities of horse manure about the Piazza San Marco. It must have been quite a feat of organisation. Perhaps Cole had brought the horse manure with him from England. Whatever the source of his supply, the people of Venice were certainly puzzled. Had there been a mysterious invasion of horses in the night? Had the dung dropped like manna from heaven? Had sea-horses emerged from the canals and dropped seahorse manure? Could it be the work of the four ancient gilt bronze equestrian statues which adorn the Piazza?

Cole, who was an inveterate hoaxer, took the peculiar view that anyone who didn't appreciate a practical joke

must be a homosexual. Perhaps this belief, combined with a determination to prove his own straightness, goes some way to explain the persistence with which he played practical jokes. It is quite possible that he was not responsible for all of the tricks he is supposed to have perpetrated. Having once gained his reputation he probably had the acts of others attributed to him, in the way that some of the witticisms quoted as those of Churchill or Oscar Wilde were in fact uttered by less celebrated contemporaries.

Was it Cole who played the famous string trick? This is the one where he stopped a respectable man in the street and asked for his help for a minute. Cole (if it was he) said that he was a surveyor whose colleague had not turned up. Would the gentleman be so kind as to hold the string for a moment while he took the other end in order to make a measurement. The gentleman kindly obliged. We must hope for his sake that this innocent was not in a hurry, for Cole then went round the corner, accosted another stranger, told the same story with the same effect, and then pushed off – leaving two complete strangers holding a piece of string and with nothing to do but look at their watches until such time as the supposed surveyor should return.

Was it Cole who was responsible for the equally well-known hole-in-the-road joke? It is supposed to have happened in one of the ancient university cities, where Cole spotted some workmen digging up the road for repairs. Cole, or whoever it was, told the workmen that he had heard that some undergraduates were planning a silly hoax. They were going to dress up as policemen and tell the roadmen to fill up the hole since they were causing an obstruction.

He then went to the police station and reported that as part of a silly hoax some undergraduates had dressed up as workmen and were digging up the road. The consequences are not hard to imagine.

Nowadays the perpetrator would be had up for every-thing from causing an affray to wasting police time. Then, however, wealthy and well-connected young university gentlemen could apparently get away with all sorts of behaviour (such as pinching policemen's helmets) which would, today get a student or football fan a fine and a lecture from the magistrate at the very least.

C.O. claimed (on what evidence I do not know) that it was Horace Cole who found himself in a railway compartment otherwise occupied only by two formidably respectable-looking ladies of a primness rarely encountered in this permissive age but not so exceptional in the period between the two World Wars. You know the kind – the ones with faces that can only register shocked disapproval. There's usually at least one in every Ealing comedy or *Carry On* film.

Cole (if it was he) sat in the middle on one side of the compartment, the ladies (who were strangers to one another) in the corner seats on the other side.

The train entered a tunnel, which Cole knew to be a long one. In those energy-saving times there was not always lighting for such occasions on day-time trains. The compartment was plunged into total darkness.

Cole made a few noisy movements in his seat. Then he kissed the back of his hand. At first quietly, and then in a more abandoned fashion, and accompanied this by low moans and murmured endearments.

When the train came out of the tunnel Cole was to be seen hurriedly straightening his tie. The two ladies spent the rest of the journey with pursed lips, exchanging extremely sharp looks.

On another occasion he successfully passed himself off as Ramsay MacDonald, whom he resembled, and in that persona made a trememdously reactionary speech to a group of trade unionists. He was equally victorious in impersonating the uncle of the Sultan of Zanzibar and in that guise successfully visited Cambridge, being formally received by the Mayor at the Guildhall, taken to a Charity Bazaar, shown the principal colleges, and given a grand send-off at the railway station. When Cole told all to the *Daily Mail*, the Mayor of Cambridge demanded of the Vice-Chancellor that Cole – together with those fellow undergraduates who had posed as his interpreter and entourage – should be sent down. However, they escaped the mayor's outrage unscathed. It can't have done much to improve Town and Gown relations.

The Sultan of Zanzibar hoax, however, was to prove only a dummy-run for Cole's most outrageous imposture. On 10 February 1910, the passengers on the train from Paddington to Weymouth included a distinguished delegation. There were six of them: the Emperor of Abyssinia, his interpreter, three retainers and a chap from the Foreign Office. They were, of course, nothing of the sort – though in their real lives they were not without genuine distinction. The dusky young man with moustache and beard, wearing a turban and a flowing embroidered caftan, was Virginia Woolf. Another black-faced, bearded, turbaned courtier was the artist Duncan Grant. Other members of the Imperial group were Adrian Stephen (Virginia's brother), Guy Ridley and Anthony Buxton. As for their Foreign Office companion in top hat and tails, this was none other than Horace de Vere Cole (characterised in Quentin Bell's account of the affair in his biography of Viginia Woolf as 'a rich and in many ways a preposterous young man').

Their object was to be given a conducted tour of the great battleship HMS *Dreadnought* – at that time the most illustrious, and therefore the most secret, fighting ship in the world – the flagship of the British Navy, no less.

It was a daunting undertaking, and they embarked on it with considerable trepidation. It was true that they had paved the way with a telegram to the Commander-in-Chief Home Fleet by a friend in the Foreign Office informing him of the arrival of the Lion of Judah, Emperor of Abyssinia, and company, but they couldn't help feeling that this might have been more convincing if it had been sent in code – something which their Foreign Office friend evidently felt would be going well beyond the call of duty. The risk of detection was made greater – much greater – by the fact that the *Dreadnought's* flag commander, whom they were almost certain to meet, was William Fisher – a cousin of Adrian and Virginia Stephen.

At Weymouth they were received with full naval ceremony. Cole (as the man from the Foreign Office) made the introductions. The bogus Emperor (Anthony Buxton) had no idea what language was spoken by the genuine article, and made do with some phrases of Swahili that he had picked up somewhere. Adrian Stephen interpreted. Cole made diplomatic noises.

A launch conveyed them to the massive *Dreadnought*, which they boarded. They inspected the Guard of Honour. Virginia Woolf shook the hand of, among many others, her cousin. She normally had a weakness for giggling, but on this occasion she managed, with difficulty, to restrain it.

As they were shown round the ship, the Emperor found that after a few remarks he had run out of Swahili and resorted to Latin. One of the junior officers was heard to remark that their foreign guest spoke a 'rum lingo'. The panic caused by this comment was compounded when they were informed that there was a member of the crew who spoke Swahili. Luckily for them he was on leave.

They were offered a meal, but declined on the grounds that their religion forbad them to eat with foreigners. The real reason was that they were worried that their greasepaint might start to run. Likewise they politely declined the honour of a twenty-one-gun salute: they feared that the reverberations might shake off their false beards. The final close shave (so to speak) came as they were leaving. The rating who was assisting Virginia Woolf into the launch was heard to remark to a shipmate, 'I say, Bill, this one's a woman.' (Which part of the anatomy he had grasped in order to discover this is not recorded.)

In spite of such close calls they managed to return to London undetected. Quentin Bell says that they had all agreed that the practical joke should not be exposed. The press should be told nothing. They had been charmingly entertained, treated in fact with such kindness that they felt rather guilty, and, at any rate, the joke had gone far enough.

If this was indeed their view they can't have known their Horace de Vere Cole. Without consulting the others he high-tailed it down to Fleet Street. The result was huge headlines in the newspapers, extremely red faces in the Royal Navy, and questions in Parliament.

Colonel Lockwood asked the First Lord of the Admiralty whether a hoax has been played upon the naval authorities by the pretended visit of some Abyssinian princes: and, if so, whether he will take steps to prevent such conduct in future?

The First Lord of the Admiralty (Mr McKenna): I understand that a number of persons have put themselves to considerable trouble and expense in pretending to be a party of Abyssinians, and in this disguise visited one of His Majesty's ships. The question is being considered whether any breach of the law has been committed which can be brought home to the offenders.

Mr William Redmond: Will the Right Hon. Gentleman include in his inquiry as to whether it is not a fact that these gentlemen conferred the Royal Abyssinian Order on the Admiral, who wrote to the King to know whether he could wear it, and will he wear it?

Mr McKenna: I shall be relieved from the necessity of inquiring into that matter because I know it not to be true.

Colonel Lockwood: Does the Right Hon. Gentleman think with me that the joke was a direct insult to His Majesty's flag?

Mr McKenna: I think I have answered the question on paper fully. The Hon. and gallant Gentleman will not ask me to go further into a matter which is obviously the work of foolish persons.

Thus *Hansard* on 24 February 1910. The matter came up again a few days later. *Hansard* 2 March 1910.

Captain Faber asked the First Lord of the Admiralty if he would state what were the circumstances which led to the giving of an official reception by the commander-in-chief, Vice Admiral Sir W. May, and the officers of HMS *Dreadnought*, to certain reputed Abyssinian princes and their staff; whether these reputed Abyssinians were received by the Admiral and the officers of the ship with full naval honours; whether by the admiral's orders they were furnished with a special train on the return journey to London; and whether an inquiry had yet been held?

The First Lord of the Admiralty (Mr McKenna): With regard to the first part of the question, I would refer the Hon. and gallant Gentleman to the reply given to the right Hon. and gallant Gentleman the Member for Epping last Thursday. No flags were hoisted or salutes fired, and no special train was ordered by the Admiral.

Captain Faber: Is it not a fact that certain pairs of white kid gloves were actually purchased for the occasion, and can the Right Hon. Gentleman say who will pay the expense?

Mr McKenna: I am afraid that the Hon. and gallant Gentleman is better informed than I am, but if he will kindly give me notice of his question I will inquire into the matter.

An appendix in Quentin Bell's biography of Virginia Woolf quotes the surviving fragment of her own account of the affair as given in a talk to the Women's Institute in Rodmell in 1940, leaving the audience (according to E.M. Forster) helpless with laughter.

We were told by a friend of Mr McKenna's that if we took all the blame on ourselves, they would not take any steps against the admiral or the other officers. The House of Commons would be told that we had apologised and there would be an end of it. So my brother and Duncan Grant went to the Admiralty and were shown in to Mr McKenna. And there they had a very queer interview. They tried to explain that they didn't want to get the admiral into trouble; and Mr McKenna dismissed the idea that such foolish people could get so great a man into a scrape, and pointed out that one of them had committed a forgery and was liable to go to gaol. So they argued at loggerheads. The truth was I think that Mr McKenna was secretly a good deal amused, and liked the hoax, but didn't want it repeated. At any rate he treated them as if they were schoolboys, and told them not to do it again. But we heard afterwards that one result of our visit had been that the regulations were tightened up; and that rules were made about telegrams that made it almost impossible now to repeat the joke. I am glad to think that I too have been of help to my country.

The First Lord of the Admiralty might take this avuncularly tolerant line, but cousins (and Willy Fisher was a cousin) are not necessarily of the kissing kind. He and his brother officers were beside themselves. In those days Britannia was still top wave-ruler, and the Senior Service's dignity had been affronted in a way that could not pass unavenged. Small boys were running after Vice-Admiral May in the street shouting 'Bunga Bunga'. Sailors in Weymouth were laughed at so much that they didn't dare go ashore. Something had to be done.

Willy Fisher decided that physical chastisement was required. With two fellow-officers he dropped in on Adrian Stephen, who escaped untouched. According to some accounts he repelled them with a poker. Others state that it was Fisher's view that naval protocol did not allow him to beat the son of his mother's sister.

He had no such inhibitions about Duncan Grant, however, who had no such blood protection. They abducted him from his house (in his bedroom slippers) and took him forcibly in a taxi to Hampstead Heath, where they told him they were going to cane him. Duncan Grant quietly submitted without resistance. Whether this was because he was a gentleman and a pacifist, or because it was pointless for him to put up a one-against-three struggle, his tactic was effective. In Virginia Woolf's account:

... this rather upset them. 'I can't make this chap out,' said one of the officers. 'He doesn't put up a fight. You can't cane a chap like that.' My cousin however ordered them to proceed. He was too high in the service to lend a hand himself. And so, very reluctantly, one of the junior officers took a cane and gave Duncan Grant two ceremonial taps. They said the honour of the navy was avenged. There was Duncan Grant standing without a hat in his bedroom slippers. They at once conceived an affection for him and I am not surprised. They were really sorry for him. 'You can't go home like that,' they said. But Duncan Grant felt that he would much rather go home in the tube in his slippers than be driven back by the officers. And so he shuffled off; and the officers disappeared in their car.

When Admiral Sir William Wordsworth Fisher died more than a quarter of a century later, Virginia Woolf wrote in a letter to Ethel Smyth: 'Yes, I'm sorry about William – our last meeting was on the deck of the *Dreadnought* in 1910, I think; but I wore a beard. And I'm afraid that he took it to heart a good deal...'

As usual Cole, the bounder, escaped unscathed.

Given Cole's behaviour, it is not surprising that his friends were very much on the *qui vive* when he was around and took all precautions to make sure that they should not number among his victims. When one of Cole's best friends was about to get married he decided that the best thing was to arrange a wedding of such formality and solemnity that even he wouldn't get up to tricks. Fat chance.

The ceremony itself went smoothly enough, with Cole in the congregation behaving as properly as anyone could wish and looking as though butter wouldn't melt in his mouth. The newly-weds left the altar, walked together down the aisle and stood outside for the photographs. At this point, a smartly dressed and extremely buxom young lady gave a shriek, threw herself on the bridegroom, clutched him in her arms and smothered him with kisses. 'Darling,' she cried, 'if this terrible thing has to happen then I wish you every happiness, but never forget the years we have spent together, and remember that when she is tired of you I will still be there waiting for you. I will wait for you forever, forever, my darling.'

Then with another anguished cry she tore herself away and made off for her next appointment − to receive a cheque from Cole.

LITERARY SUPPLEMENTS

C.O. was not a great reader, except in areas which involved his highly specialised interest. This sometimes took him into fairly obscure regions, normally trampled on only by literary scholars. For example, he knew more about James Macpherson (born in Invernesshire in 1736, died 1796) than anyone else I have met (apart, of course, from Dr Peter Hogg-Strangeways, who knows about little else).

Macpherson claimed to have found, and to have collected from the oral tradition, works of the semi-legendary third-century poet Ossian, and at the age of 26 he published *Fragments of Ancient Poetry Collected in the Highlands of Scotland, and Translated from the Gallic or Erse Language* (1760). This work was greeted with such acclaim that a public subscription was raised to finance his further researches, resulting in the publication of *Fingal: An Ancient Epic Poem, Temora* (1763) and *The Works of Ossian* (in two volumes 1765).

One of the first to cast doubt on the authenticity of these works was Samuel Johnson. Boswell says that he does not know the precise words used by Macpherson in his angry letter to 'the venerable Sage' but that he understands that the language used was 'of a nature very different from the language of literary contest'. Johnson's reply showed him at his dignified and fearless best.

MR JAMES MACPHERSON

I received your foolish and impudent letter. Any violence offered me I shall do my best to repel; and what I cannot do for myself, the law shall do for me. I hope I shall never be deterred from detecting what I think a cheat, by the menaces of a ruffian. What would you have me retract? I thought your book an imposture; I think it an imposture still. For this opinion I have given my reasons to the public, which I here dare you to refute. Your rage I defy. Your abilities, since your Homer, are not so formidable; and what I hear of your morals, inclines me to pay regard not to what you shall say, but to what you shall prove. You may print this if you will.

SAM JOHNSON

There were many less perspicacious people who did not share Johnson's view that the Ossian works were 'impudent forgeries', and Macpherson's works were acclaimed with especial enthusiasm on the Continent, then suffering from an acute seizure of romanticism. Though Macpherson was never able to produce the manuscripts he claimed to have found, his reputation defied even Johnson's contempt and he managed to get himself buried in Westminster Abbey.

Some people still think highly of Macpherson's *Ossian*, whether it was a forgery or not. This is commonly the upshot of literary and artistic hoaxes. In order to carry off this kind of thing you have to produce something which is really quite good. Thomas Chatterton (1752-70) is a classic example.

He was born in Bristol, the posthumous son of a schoolmaster who deserves to be remembered, not just as the father of a celebrated son but also for his mouth, which was so wide that he could put his clenched fist in it.

Chatterton was a poet endowed with a facility matched only by his financial poverty. The combination caused him to put his undoubted talents to ends which were not entirely legal. He cooked up some bogus poems purporting to be the work of an invented fifteenth-century poet called Thomas Rowley. He also concocted a history of painting in England by Rowley, and a number of other supposedly ancient poems and documents. Chatterton managed to get these published, but the fraud was soon exposed in T. Tyrwhitt's *Poems supposed to have been written by Thomas Rowley.* Chatterton is a tragic case. Though his poems are fakes, they were at the same time poems of a high order in their own right. Dragged down by poverty, unable to make money from his pen either legally or illegally, he poisoned himself with arsenic. He was 17.

The borderline between fakes, forgeries and frauds on the one hand and hoaxes and practical jokes on the other is a bit blurred. There is a grey area in the middle. Or so it seems to me. C.O., however, was not too worried about this. Macpherson and Chatterton (and indeed Clifford Irving, the author of the bogus Howard Hughes autobiography) were hoaxers; but they were also forgers, fakers and frauds – or were they practical jokers? Clearly C.O. saw them as the latter, which is why they found themselves in his files. I'm not quite sure. I wouldn't be surprised to learn that C.O.'s disappearance was not unconnected with his failure to discriminate on this point.

Still, C.O.'s archives do contain examples of literary hoaxes which very definitely are practical jokes rather than frauds. Those of Jonathan Swift for example. It is said that Swift could remember having laughed only twice in his life (unfortunately there is no record of what occasioned these rare outbreaks of mirth). It was part of Swift's great comic gift that he could keep a completely straight face. *Gulliver's Travels* itself is in a sense a hoax, for its title page claims it to be a genuine account of 'Travels into Several Remote Nations of the World ... By Lemuel

Gulliver, first a Surgeon, and then a Captain of several ships'. When it was published many people took it to be authentic. One reader who was not taken in was a distinguished prelate who announced that he didn't believe a word of it: he had consulted an atlas and found that there were no such places as Lilliput and Brobdingnag.

Swift's most elaborate joke was at the expense of a cobbler turned astrologer and almanac-maker by the name of John Partridge (1644-1715), who published an annual volume of predictions, *Merlinus Liberatus*. This was the *Old Moore's Almanac* of its day. Amongst other things it included much abuse of competitors in the prediction business, as well as advertisements for quack medicines. Partridge's predictions, in the judicious words of the *Dictionary of National Biography*, carried 'the phraseology of equivocation . . . to a pitch of rare perfection'. Such was Swift's victim.

At almanac time in 1707, simultaneously with Partridge's *Merlinus Liberatus* for the year, there appeared a rival almanac entitled *Predictions for the year 1708 . . . written to prevent the people of England from being further imposed upon by vulgar almanac makers* by Isaac Bickerstaff Esq.

Bickerstaff (a name Swift had taken from a shop-front) gravely announced that his intention was to rescue astrology from the abuses of illiterate impostors. Whereas *their* predictions were vague and ambiguous, *his* were precise. For example, he predicted the exact date and time of the death of John Partridge, almanac-maker. 'I have consulted the star of his nativity by my own rule, and find he will infallibly die upon 29 March next, about 11 at night, of a raging fever.'

Bickerstaff's predictions were followed by a heated refutation: *Answer to Bickerstaff: some Reflections upon Mr Bickerstaff's Predictions for the year* by 'A person of quality'. This too was by Swift. Public interest began to rise.

Bickerstaff had predicted that Partridge would die on 29 March. On 30 March was published (presumably for sale on 1 April) a pamphlet (Swift again) entitled *The Accomplishment of the first of Mr Bickerstaff's Predictions, being an account of the death of Mr Partridge the almanack-maker upon the 29th inst*. The deathbed scene was described in detail, complete with Partridge's dying confession that he was an impostor. The pamphlet also had the honesty to admit that Mr Bickerstaff had been a full four hours out in his prediction.

The pamphlet was widely bought, read and discussed. Swift heaped fuel onto the already blazing fire with an 'Elegy on the Death of Mr Partridge'. It concludes with the epitaph:

> Here, five feet deep, lies on his back
> A cobbler, starmonger, and quack,
> Who to the stars in pure good will
> Does to his best look upward still:
> Weep, all you customers that use
> His pills, his almanacks, or shoes.

On learning that Partridge was dead, the Company of Stationers, which controlled publishing at that time, ordered that his name should be removed from their rolls, and asked for an injunction preventing further almanacs from being published in his name. In far-off Portugal the Inquisition learned of Bickerstaff's uncannily accurate prediction and ordered that his works should be burnt since they must certainly be the work of the devil.

Meanwhile the wretched Partridge was vainly trying to establish that he was still alive. On 2 April he wrote to the postmaster in Ireland: 'I don't doubt but you are imposed on in Ireland also by a pack of rogues about my being dead.' Unluckily for Partridge, the postmaster, Isaac Manley, was a friend of Swift's, and to Partridge's increased discomfort his letter also found its way into print.

Partridge's attempts to prove that he was not dead soon had London in stitches. Swift milked the last drop from the joke with his pamphlet *Vindication of Isaac Bickerstaff Esq., against what is objected to him by Mr Partridge in his Almanack for the present year, 1709* in which he gravely states the absurdity of Partridge's pretence to be still alive. Nor did Partridge make things easier for himself by taking out an advertisement in the newspapers announcing that not only was he alive 'but was also alive upon the 29th March in question.'

A more private Swiftian joke was played when he was employed as chaplain to Lord Berkeley. One of the chores involved in this job was to read to Lady Berkeley from Robert Boyle's *Meditations*, a work which Swift did not admire. Swift wrote a parody of Boyle, 'A Meditation on a Broomstick', in which he makes all sorts of far-fetched comparisons between a broomstick and humankind (rather in the manner which is still to be heard most mornings on Radio 4's Thought for the Day). It begins:

This single Stick, which you now behold Ingloriously lying in that neglected Corner, I once knew in a Flourishing State in A Forest, it was full of Sap, full of Leaves, and full of Boughs, but now, in vain, does the busie Art of Man pretend to Vye with Nature, by tying that wither'd Bundle of Twigs to its sapless Trunk; 'tis now at best but the Reverse of what it was, a Tree turn'd upside down, the Branches on the Earth, and the Root in the air; ... when I beheld this, I sigh'd, and said within myself, Surely Man is a Broomstick ...

Swift inserted this parody into the volume of Boyle's works and replaced it on the bookshelf. The next time Lady Berkeley felt the need for some Boyle, Swift opened the book and solemnley read out the words 'A Meditation on a Broomstick'. Lady Berkeley was surprised by this odd title. 'A meditation on a Broomstick!' she exclaimed. 'What a strange subject! But there is no knowing what useful lessons of instruction this wonderful man may draw from things apparently the most trivial. Pray let us hear what he says upon it.'

Thomas Sheridan, Swift's biographer and the father of the dramatist, says that Swift then 'with an inflexible gravity of countenance, proceeded to read the meditation, in the same solemn tone which he had used in delivering the former. Lady Berkeley, not at all suspecting a trick, in the fulness of her prepossession, was every now and then, during the reading of it, expressing her admiration of this extraordinary man, who could draw such fine moral reflections from so contemptible a subject. With which, though Swift must have been inwardly not a little tickled, yet he preserved a most perfect composure of features...'

When the hoax was revealed Lady Berkeley had the sense to take it in good part, commenting only, 'What a vile trick that rogue played on me. But it is his way, he never balks his humour in anything.'

C.O. Jones reckoned that it was as perfect as a practical joke could be. For one thing, it made a point, which was to ridicule the moralisings of Robert Boyle. It was also in itself a brilliant piece of parody: in his excellent anthology of parodies, Dwight Macdonald says that it is the first parody that imitates the thought as well as the style of the

victim, and that it is of a quality not to have been reached for more than a hundred years. Furthermore it caused suffering to no-one, and was carried out with an impeccably straight face. The combination of Swift's 'perfect composure of features' with his being 'inwardly not a little tickled' is as good an image of the practical joker as one could hope to find.

Swift's friend Alexander Pope was a fairly prickly character, a fact which others did not fail to turn to advantage. One day Pope was reading to Swift the passage of *The Rape of the Lock* that he had just completed. This was in confidence, because Pope was always worried about pirated editions of his work and didn't want anything to get out ahead of publication. It so happened that a friend, Thomas Parnell, overheard the reading. Being gifted with an extraordinary memory, Parnell was able to recall the entire passage on this single reading. He then translated it into Latin.

Shortly afterwards Pope read the passage to a group of friends, who enjoyed it enormously. Parnell, choosing his moment carefully, then produced what appeared to be an old Latin manuscript, from which he proceeded to read. The result was that Pope's lines appeared to be at best translation, at worst a work of plagiarism. It took Pope some time to discover the truth. He didn't take it at all well.

Wordsworth is probably the most parodied of all great poets. In Dwight Macdonald's anthology of parodies, he scores twelve entries: Browning comes second with nine. Wordsworth – 'that pedlar-praising son of a bitch' in Byron's phrase – is so easy to parody that he often did so himself, though not intentionally. For example:

The beetle loves his unpretending track,
The snail the house he carries on his back,
The far-fetched worm with pleasure would disown
The bed we give him, though of softest down.
(Liberty)

But even if Wordsworth *is* easy to parody, one's hat has to be taken off to John Hamilton Reynolds who published a parody of *Peter Bell* before the real thing had come out. Reynolds had contrived to catch a glimpse of the manuscript at the printers and is said to have dashed off his version in a single day. It begins:

> It is the thirty-first of March
> A gusty evening .. half past seven;
> The moon is shining o'er the larch,
> A simple shape .. a cock'd-up arch,
> Rising bigger than a star,
> Though the stars are thick in Heaven

The poet meets a suitably Wordsworthian rustic:

> Beneath the ever blessed moon
> An old man o'er an old grave stares.
> You never look'd upon his fellow;
> His brow is covered with grey hairs,
> As though they were an umbrella.

Needless to say who this gnarled old chap is:

> 'Tis Peter Bell .. 'tis Peter Bell,
> Who never stirreth in the day;
> His hand is wither'd .. he is old;
> On Sundays he is us'd to pray,
> In winter he is very cold.

Hamilton provides a footnote on the subject of Peter Bell's coldness: 'Peter Bell resembleth Harry Gill in this particular: "His teeth they chatter, chatter, chatter". I should have introduced this fact in the text, but that Harry Gill would not rhyme. I reserve this for my blank verse.' Hamilton goes on to saw away at Peter Bell's family tree.

> He is rurally related;
> Peter hath country cousins,
> (He had once a worthy mother)
> Bells and Peters by the dozens,
> But Peter Bell he hath no brother.

Not a brother owneth he,
Peter Bell he hath no brother,
His mother had no other son,
No other son e'er call'd her mother;
Peter Bell hath brother none.

Hamilton's *Peter Bell* ran to 42 verses, to which was added a preface signed W.W.:

It is now a period of one-and-twenty years since I first wrote some of the most perfect compositions (except certain pieces I have written in my later days) that ever dropped from poetical pen. It has been my aim and my achievement to deduce moral thunder from buttercups, daisies, celandines, and (as a poet scarcely inferior to myself hath it) 'such small deer'. Out of sparrows' eggs I have hatched great truths, and with sextons' barrows have I wheeled into human hearts piles of the weightiest philosophy.

It was the existence of the two *Peter Bells* (Wordsworth's own, preceded by Hamilton's bogus one) that caused Shelley to call *his* parody *Peter Bell the Third*. It wasn't very good, lacking both Reynold's wit and the venom of Byron's 'Epilogue', which goes:

There's something in a stupid ass:
And something in a heavy dunce;
But never since I went to school
I saw or heard so damned a fool
As William Wordsworth is for once.

And now I've seen so great a fool
As William Wordsworth is for once,
I really wish that Peter Bell
And he who wrote it were in hell,
For writing nonsense for the nonce.

Wordsworth was not amused by the parodies, and replied with yet another Wordsworth parody (unintentional, of course).

A book came forth of late called *Peter Bell*;
Not negligent the style; the matter ? good
As aught that song records of Robin Hood . . .

Whatever else Wordsworth can be accused of, he was certainly innocent of a sense of humour.

The short stories of Guy de Maupassant (1850-1893) frequently end with a twist in the tail of a kind that make it no surprise to learn that the author was adept at contriving such situations in real life. Maupassant was, in short, a considerable practical joker, and actually wrote a book called *Memoirs of a Joker* (1883). In this he tells of many tricks that he carried out, or that were played on him. From C.O.'s underscorings and the copious marginal notes in his own copy of Maupassant's book, it would appear that he particularly relished the following joke.

During the course of one especially pleasant autumn, Maupassant went to stay with some friends for a hunting weekend at a country house in Picardy. Since they *were* his friends, he knew them to be keen practical jokers. Therefore he was on his guard from the start. On arrival he was given a hugely effusive welcome. Was it not too effusive? He was more suspicious than ever.

It was the same during dinner, Maupassant records. Everyone was in high spirits, but he couldn't help thinking they were *too* high. His friends laughed at his jokes, which was gratifying, but they laughed too long. Clearly something

was up, and it was something he wasn't in on. They were trying to get him in a good mood, lulling him into a sense of false security. In short, they were setting him up. Nothing untoward had occurred, but he was determined not to be caught. He said nothing but suspected everyone from his hosts and fellow-guests to the servants.

At bedtime everyone accompanied him to his room. Why? He entered the room, shut the door, and heard stifled laughter outside. What was up? Something, clearly. He made a minute inspection of the walls, furniture, curtains, chest-of-drawers, wardrobe, carpet and everything else without finding anything the slightest bit odd. Finally he sat down, with great trepidation, expecting a howl of laughter from outside. The chair held.

Time passed. Maupassant thought. Nothing happened. Finally he decided to go to bed. The bed! That must be it. Although his thorough inspection had revealed nothing, it was obvious that whatever was going to happen had to do with the bed. Something like a bucket of cold water dropping from above. Well, he was determined to out-fox them.

He took the mattress and bedclothes and settled down for the night, as best he could, on the floor in the middle of the room. He lay awake for an hour, bristling at the slightest sound, ever alert for some disaster to overtake him and for his friends to burst into his room to enjoy the fun. Finally sleep overtook him.

He was awoken very suddenly, by someone falling heavily on him; at the same time he heard a tremendous crashing of crockery and received on his person a quantity of painfully hot liquid.

What had happened was that the servant bringing him his morning tea had tripped over the makeshift bed in the middle of the room. Maupassant's over-careful precautions had caused him to be the victim of a practical joke that never existed.

Presumably the French don't have a phrase meaning,

'hoist with his own petard'; otherwise Maupassant's narrative would surely have ended by using it. C.O.'s annotations include an award to this incident of 9 points out of 10 as a self-inflicted practical joke.

A literary definition of one of the most popular and time-tested of practical jokes is given in the *Shorter Oxford Dictionary*, where an apple-pie bed is described as one 'in which, as a practical joke, the sheets are so folded that a person cannot get his legs down'. (I'm digressing somewhat here, though the connection between this hoary practical joke and a reference in C.O. Jones's notes to one of the century's most eminent writers will become apparent in a page or so.) Anyway ... the *Shorter Oxford Dictionary*'s definition, like so many dictionary entries, is not very helpful. If you already know what an apple-pie bed is, you can see what they mean. But then, if you already know what an apple-pie bed is you hardly need to look it up. If you don't know, it doesn't enlighten you. A Martian reading this dictionary entry would be puzzled as to how a bed could be so made that a person could not get his legs down. Why were the person's legs up in the first place?

A Martian, or an American. C.O. Jones once pointed out to me that apple-pie beds are unknown in the United States. I challenged this theory, whereupon he produced yet another dictionary, which specifically noted that apple-pie bed – 'a way of making a bed so as to prevent a person from entering it' – is an exclusively British term.

In order to put this theory to the test, I embarked – with C.O.'s connivance – on a piece of research made possible by the imminent arrival of some guests from America. In anticipation of their short stay, my co-operation was requested in the service of bed-making. Now, as it happens, bed-making is something I normally never get mixed up in. I just never make beds. For myself, I am prepared to sleep under a jumble of sheets and blankets. If other people insist on their beds being arranged in a more orderly manner, then that is up to them. Other domestic duties I will carry out cheerfully (or grumpily). I will wash up the dishes, feed the cat, put up bookshelves, even un-block drains. But I won't make beds. Except apple-pie ones. Since the American guests included two children, I volunteered to make their beds (and their beds only). I performed this task in the only way I know how – that is to say, in apple-pie fashion.

For the benefit of Americans and other ignorant people the procedure is as follows.

1. Spread the bottom sheet, and tuck in all round.
2. Spread the top sheet, tucking in the top and the upper parts of the sides.
3. Place the pillow on top of the *top* sheet.
4. Fold back the top sheet to cover the pillow.
5. Add blankets to taste in the normal manner. Fold back the top of the top sheet (which is in fact the bottom of the top sheet, if you follow me). Tuck in bed clothes all round and *voilà*.

The American guests arrived and in due course the children went to bed. Surprisingly there was no reaction. It turned out that the girl simply curled up and slept at the top of the bed. The boy's only comment the next morning was a whispered remark to his mother: 'They sure make beds funny in England.'

C.O. Jones once drew my attention, by the way, to a

variation on the apple-pie bed that is popular (for reasons that escape me) in the French army. You place a bottle of cold water between the sheets. Finding it there the victim will merely remove it. Repeat the operation the next night. And again on the third, but this time take a piece of string and tie it to the cork of the bottle. The other end of the string is tied to the foot of the bed. The exasperated owner of the bed, if things go according to plan, will forcibly remove the bottle from the bed, and the cork from the bottle, thereby releasing a flood of cold water.

The subject of apple-pie beds brings us (as I promised it would) to a literary notable, Max Beerbohm, of all unlikely people, who was still making apple-pie beds well into his fifties. It is not the age which is so surprising. Rather it is that one had never imagined that such an immensely dandified figure ever made a bed of any kind at all. Once one has got over that shock, the rest is understandable. Whether he ever made an ordinary bed in his fifties, or before or after, is not recorded.

His practical jokes (according to his biographer Lord David Cecil) were more usually designed to disconcert the mind rather than (as with apple-pie beds) the body. Lord David tells us that on one occasion Max altered all the labels in a lady's rose garden. She and some visiting guests were greatly puzzled to find that all her roses were named after famous criminals ... Betty Uprichard had become Dr Crippen, and so on.

He was especially keen on playing jokes involving books, and he performed them with characteristic meticulousness. One of these was inflicted on a volume of exceptionally solemn poems by a dullard called Herbert Trench. This collection included a romantic dialogue between Apollo and a mariner. With a sharp knife and painstaking care Max scraped out the aspirates at the beginning of every word beginning with 'h' spoken by the mariner, and substituted an apostrophe. The result was that a speech intended to be of classical dignity was turned into straight Cockney. Max then sent the book to the author, commenting that he had not previously come across this edition of the book.

The work had been done so carefully that it appeared to be perfectly genuine. At first Trench was horrified. When he tumbled, he was offended. Max made it up by explaining to Trench that he considered him to be a true poet – 'Otherwise there wouldn't be any fun in making fun of you.'

One of his more elaborate jokes was at the expense of George Bernard Shaw. Discovering a book of photographs of the dramatist as a young man, Max carefully altered them all for the worse: making the nose bigger in one, giving the eyes a squint in another, and so on. He then had these re-photographed and sent them to various friends with the request that they should send them to Shaw as though from a fan, asking for the photograph to be signed and returned. Shaw was much perplexed.

Visitors to Max's library would find some extremely odd books on his shelves. *The Love Poems of Herbert Spencer*, for example, or a very slim volume entitled *The Complete Works of Arnold Bennett*: whatever the philosopher Herbert Spencer may have been his reputation was hardly that of an amorous poet, and whatever else may be said about Arnold Bennett he was nothing if not prolific. Visitors curious enough to take down these volumes found them to be wooden dummies.

At whatever age he may have stopped making apple-pie beds, Max continued his joke books to the end of his long life. He would spend days, weeks, months, sometimes years, in 'improving' books, making a subtle change to the title-page here, altering an illustration caption there, or writing forged dedications or messages to the author such as the one found in Max's copy of Ibsen's plays. It reads, in Ibsen's handwriting and Norwenglish:

> For Max Beerbohm
> critic of who
> the writings fills
> with pleasures me.   H. Ibsen

In Max's copy of Queen Victoria's *More Leaves from the Journal of a Life in the Highlands*, all the illustrations are subtly and delicately altered, and the text has comments in the Queen's handwriting and characteristic literary style. Thus, under a picture of the Queen's dog, Sharp, is written: 'Such a dear, faithful, noble *friend* and companion, and for whom Albert had the greatest respect also. Victoria R.'

At the beginning of the book there is a dedication:

> For Mr Beerbohm
> the never-sufficiently-
> to-be-studied writer
> whom Albert looks
> down on affectionately,
> I am sure . .
> From his Sovereign   Victoria R.I.
> Balmoral, 1898

Many analysts and critics have concluded that humour contains an element (at least) of aggression, and one would not have to be a fully paid-up follower of Sigmund's to come up with the idea that practical jokers are sublimated sadists. (Note to the Reader: Don't worry, this bit isn't going to last long.) Plato considered laughter to be 'a malicious gloating over the misfortunes of others'. For Hobbes laughter is 'nothing else but sudden glory arising from a sudden conception of some eminency in ourselves, by comparison with the infirmity of others, or with our own formerly'. Certainly racist, nationalistic and sexist jokes of the kind men cackle at in pubs are aggressive, and it would be easy to argue that practical jokes are too, since their very purpose is to set up a victim and bring him down.

Beerbohm's example is an exception which disproves the rule. For one thing he is funniest when dealing with subjects for which he has affection. For another, he seems to have played many of his jokes purely for his own amusement and not for the discomfiture of anyone else. Many of them remained undiscovered in his library, unknown not only to the victim but also to anyone else. Some of them came to light only years after his death, such as those found only a few years ago in the books of a friend he stayed with in exile from Rappallo during the war. Doubtless more remain, waiting to be discovered and to explode. They were done not in a spirit of malice but of fun and sheer playfulness. Joke for joke's sake, one might say. C.O. Jones used to say that if he had to choose a First Eleven of practical jokers Max would be an automatic choice. C.O. saw Max in practical joking terms as a bowler of googlies. Personally I find the idea of Max doing anything as energetic as playing cricket hard to imagine. Still, one gets the point.

C.O. collected a number of such examples of practical jokes involving literary figures. His favourite was the story of the Australian poet Ern Malley.

During the Second World War there existed an Australian literary magazine called *Angry Penguins*. In spite of this somewhat improbable name the magazine enjoyed a high reputation amongst the small population that comprised the Australian literati, who considered *Angry Penguins* something of a pace-setter for the avant-garde. The

distinguished artist Sidney Nolan was closely associated with it, and the editor was a respected literary figure called Max Harris.

Angry Penguins saw its function as that of a propagandist for the modern movement in literature, a task which in the Australia of that time must have been like trying to sell whisky to Mormons, or contraceptives to the Vatican. However, the opposition to *Angry Penguins* came not only from the ranks of indifferent or mocking Philistines. There were certain members of the minuscule Australian literary scene who, for different reasons, were also not too enamoured with what Max Harris and his magazine were doing. They felt that perhaps *Angry Penguins* was just a little bit *too* receptive to modernist literature.

In 1944 Max Harris received a letter from a Miss Ethel Malley in which she said that while going through the effects of her late brother, Ern Malley, she had come across a number of poems. She was no judge of poetry herself but she had shown them to various people whose opinions on such matters she respected. They had considered that the

poems were not without merit, and she enclosed a few in the hope that the editors of *Angry Penguins* would be able to spare some of their valuable time in passing judgement on them.

Harris read the poems and considered them to be brilliant. He entered into a correspondence with Ethel Malley, from which it was revealed that she was middle-class, middle-brow and middle-aged. It also emerged that her deceased brother (born 1918) had worked as a motor-mechanic in Sydney, and as an insurance salesman and watch-repairer in Melbourne. Miss Malley later sent a further batch of poems and some aphoristic prose paragraphs, one of which was a comment by the poet on his own work. It reads as follows: 'These poems are complete in themselves. They have a domestic economy of their own. If they face outwards to the reader it is because they have first faced inwards to themselves. Every poem should be an autocracy.'

Harris evidently agreed about the completeness of the poems, and came to the conclusion that he had discovered a literary genius whose career had been interrupted in as cruel and untimely a manner as those of Keats and Wilfred Owen. Accordingly, in autumn 1944, Harris devoted a whole issue of *Angry Penguins* to publishing the complete works of Ern Malley. It came out under the title *The Darkening Ecliptic*, with a cover by Sidney Nolan.

Harris hoped he was making literary history, and indeed that issue of *Angry Penguins* is now a collector's item. Ern Malley became one of the best-known poets that Australia has produced, though not exactly for the reasons that Harris had published him. It turned out that Ern's life works had been cobbled together by two young airmen in Victoria Barracks in one Saturday afternoon with the assistance of a few standard books, (such as a dictionary and the works of Shakespeare) from which they selected words and phrases haphazardly.

Harold Stewart and James Macaulay were both later to become established poets in their own right, though the fame of neither of them has been anything like that of Ern. After the hoax came out into the open, they claimed that it was a serious literary experiment intended to demonstrate that devotees of the poetical fashion of the time were insensible to absurdity and incapable of ordinary discrimination. They were trying to see whether people could tell the difference between a poem and a collection of words, and whether critics and readers still retained a sense of beauty and a sense of humour.

They claimed that the bogusness of the poems ought to have been immediately obvious to any careful reader. The first three lines of one poem were taken straight from a Government Report on the drainage of breeding-grounds of mosquitoes. Stewart and Macaulay thought it should have been obvious that the quotation from Lenin – 'The emotions are not skilled workers' – was a fabrication. And surely the editor, Max Harris, should have been alerted by the lines 'In the twenty-fifth year of my age/I find myself to be a dromedary'.

The hoax had all sorts of results that cannot have been anticipated by its perpetrators. First of all it received attention far beyond the readership of a small literary magazine. The Australian press took it up in a big way, as welcome relief from the normal coverage of war-time news. The public attention was intensified by a ridiculous prosecution of Harris for publishing indecent matter in the Ern Malley poems. One of these was about a young couple in a park after nightfall. A policeman gave evidence that this made the poem indecent, immoral and obscene on the grounds that in his considerable experience young people go into the park after dark for only one reason.

After a three-day trial Harris was fined a fiver. This was not a huge financial penalty, and in fact helped Harris considerably. One of the rules that Stewart and Macaulay had imposed on themselves was that the poems should have no coherent theme (another was that no care should be taken over verse technique, apart from vaguely imitating the currently fashionable forms of such poets as Dylan Thomas). Since the jury had found the poems to be obscene, after the court's leisurely analysis of them line by line, it was apparently established in law that the poems were not meaningless, and that Stewart and Macaulay had therefore failed in their attempt to be incoherent.

This view was shared by a number of highly distinguished literary figures, from T.S. Eliot to Sir Herbert Read, who argued that Stewart and Macaulay had been hoist by their own petard since they had accidentally touched off unconscious sources of inspiration.

Stewart and Macaulay both went on to produce distinguished work under their own names, but there are still many readers who reckon that their best productions are the ones written under the name of Ern Malley, a fact which can't have gratified them any more than Max Harris can have been pleased at being hoaxed. In an Australian radio programme by John Thompson in 1961, Stewart quoted (in support of his argument that he and Macaulay had written consciously contrived nonsense) the dromedary lines:

> In the twenty-fifth year of my age
> I find myself to be a dromedary

This certainly sounds ridiculous, but Stewart wasn't playing entirely fair. What Ern Malley actually wrote was:

> In the twenty-fifth year of my age
> I find myself to be a dromedary
> That has run short of water
> Between one oasis and the next mirage.

At least I think that's what he wrote. The reason I'm not sure is that I have not read the poem but only heard it on Thompson's radio programme. Nevertheless, I am willing to bet that I've got the line-breaks in the right places, which means that there is more verse technique than the jokers intended. Furthermore, the first line has a respectable literary pedigree going back through Ezra Pound to Villon. The image of the parched animal between oasis and mirage is not at all bad, while Lenin's aphorism about the emotions not being skilled workers is really rather good. There is certainly a case to be argued that Ern Malley's poems are considerably better than Stewart and Macaulay ever intended them to be.

Still, they undeniably caused some red faces among the trendy litterateurs of the day. Critics of Stewart and Macaulay accused them of irresponsibly providing ammunition for the anti-art, anti-intellectual Philistines of the day. But, as Peter Porter (himself a distinguished poet of Australian origin) commented to me recently, providing ammunition to the Philistines in the Australia of the 1940s was like trying to add sugar to a saturated solution.

Perhaps it was appropriate that an Australian practical joke should have turned out to be a boomerang. Stewart and Macaulay had decently decided from the start that they should not make financial gain out of the hoax. Accordingly they had made Ethel Malley give *Angry Penguins* the full copyright of her late brother's poems. Harris and his co-editors have subsequently re-published Ern's works many times and received a financial return which must in some measure have compensated for their embarrassment.

In recent years the most fashionable and most controversial of literary theories has been structuralism, an approach which has been imported from the EEC at the very time that the people who begin at Calais started to lose interest in it. The same happened with the New Wave in the cinema, the *nouveau roman* in fiction and the *nouvelle cuisine* in the kitchen.

Last year on Radio 3 Malcolm Bradbury gave a talk which should have helped us all to catch up on what he described as a neglected classic of structuralism. By way of introduction he described structuralism as a tendency, or thought-movement', which offered a post-Marxist and post-Freudian synthesis, 'an anthropology and sociology of contemporary as well as past societies, a massive, interdisciplinary tactic for exploring through language, exchange and mutuality the entirety of a cultural structure, the way every act is nominally bonded into every act.'

Bradbury's neglected structuralist masterpiece is Henri Mensonge's first book, *La fornication comme un acte culturel*, shortly to be published in English by Jonathan Cape Ltd. under the rather more timid title *Sex and Culture*. In this semiotic (indeed seminal) book, Mensonge takes fornication as culture's metaphorical centre, opening an entirely new field of iconoclastic enquiry.

In spite of the fact that in French *mensonge* means falsehood, fib or lie, and in spite still of the fact that Professor Bradbury's talk was broadcast on 1 April, it was received in total silence. Perhaps that's not so surprising, since no one is quite sure how seriously the structuralists and semiologists actually take themselves. Very, I suspect, but it's hard to be sure. While I have been typing out the above words (on Monday 6 July 1981) I have also been half-listening to the radio commentary on the Lord's Test Match. In one of the breaks between overs Trevor Bailey has just read out a letter from a lecturer in linguistics at Cambridge University, pointing out that the score of 111 visually resembles the form of the wicket, and that (in the language of semiotics) this is a remarkable example of 'iconicity'. No wonder Malcolm Bradbury's spoof went unremarked by the listeners of Radio 3. It is one subject on which it would be interesting to have the views of the History Man.

I've already mentioned, however, that C.O. Jones was not a great lover of literature, except where it in some way had to do with practical jokes, hoaxes, spoofs or frauds. In fact, I can only recall one instance of his having visited bookshops, and that was for the sole purpose of distributing dummy copies of a tome, fabricated by himself and bearing a luridly coloured jacket which bore the title *Pornography for the Young*. Apparently, he managed to find prominent display-space for this startling volume in some fifty or so bookshops during the course of a week's travelling around London and the Home Counties. Among his boxes of notes and clippings were some interesting pieces concerning the activities of various Watch Committees in the areas C.O. had visited.

His indifference to literature, though, was as nothing compared to his attitude to music. C.O. freely admitted to being tone deaf; he also considered that anyone who could find enjoyment in popular music was probably suffering from brain damage and that lovers of the classics and opera were victims of peer-group pressure. Even so, he was not a man to discriminate if music entered the realms of practical joking. If, during the course of a dinner party for example, the conversation should turn to music, C.O. would nip in the bud any pretentious exposition on the merits of a new rock-and-roll band or dissertation on some atonal jolter of crotchets and semi-quavers, by trotting out one of his musical jokes.

There were two that I particularly liked. The first concerned Mozart and Haydn: rivals and contemporaries of course. It appears that Mozart once offered Haydn a bet that he couldn't play the piece that he (Mozart) had just composed. Haydn accepted the bet and sat down at the keyboard with the music. He had only to glance at it to see that it was indeed unplayable. At a point when both hands were fully extended and far apart, a note had to be played in the middle. Either this was impossible or Mozart had made a mistake. Not so. Mozart showed him how to do it. At the required moment he ducked his head and struck the key with his nose.

The second story, C.O. would point out, had less to do with technique than with equipment, and for that reason possessed a more general application – something of which C.O. approved. He was always looking for instances of practical jokes that could be adapted to various situations or disciplines.

Joe Venuti, jazz violinist of the late 1920s, once hired a bass player for a gig, telling the musician to turn up at ten o'clock in the morning on a particular corner of a particular street with his bulky instrument. Nothing very unusual about that. But what Venuti did was to hire another bass player to turn up at the same time and place. And another.

And another. In all he hired forty bass players. At the appointed time he hired a cab, which he ordered to be driven round the area while he enjoyed what must have been really rather a remarkable spectacle. In fairness to Venuti it should be added that he paid all the musicians for the day's work, which attests to his sense of fair play. Although C.O. thoroughly approved of Venuti's sense of finesse in choosing bass-players as opposed to flautists or trumpeters (C.O. of course, would have picked timpanists) he did feel that the jazzman had softened unnecessarily in stumping up their day's pay. Victims, in C.O.'s view, are born that way and to compensate them is rather to miss the point.

One other snippet of musical information among C.O.'s notes mystified me for a while. It referred to the enormous new *Groves Dictionary of Music and Musicians* which runs to 20 volumes, over 22,000 entries, several million words, and is a snip at £950. The first edition includes an entry on the Danish composer Esrum-Hellerup, written by BBC music talks producer Robert Layton, who also wrote the entries on Sibelius and various other Scandinavian composers. C.O. hadn't elucidated on this, so I did some elementary detective work. To my delight, I discovered that the difference between Esrum-Hellerup and the subjects of Layton's other contributions is that Esrum-Hellerup is the name of a Danish railway line.

ALL THE WORLD'S A STAGE

C.O. Jones was not a great theatre-goer. By and large he was more inclined to make his own 'entertainment', as those acquainted with him often discovered to their cost. He was, though, a great admirer of those in the profession who shared with him a love of the practical joke, the spoof, the hoax.

Actors are much given to practical joking, particularly during very long runs of not frightfully good plays. The temptation to relieve the monotony of daily and sometimes twice-daily repetition of the same boring words and actions must at times become irresistible, and it is not rare for an actor with his back to the audience to pull a comic face at another player in the hope that he or she will 'corpse' – that is to say, be forced into involuntary laughter. Peter Sellers was notorious for corpsing while filming, and just as frequently he caused other actors to do so.

This happened so often on one of the Pink Panther films that the constant re-takes began to have a serious delaying effect on the shooting schedule. In desperation the film's director Blake Edwards (who was just as guilty as anyone else) slapped down a fiver, announcing that it was for charity, and that in future anyone corpsing would have to add another fiver to it.

Sellers had soon made many charitable contributions, as had the other actors, cameramen, lighting-men and the rest of the crew, all except Sellers' co-star, George Sanders, who was not only stony-faced but also extremely mean. Sanders was determined not to fork out a fiver. Evidently Sellers was equally determined that he should.

It was this situation that prompted one of Sellers' most notable jokes. Inspector Clouseau's assault on the English language had become increasingly wild as one Panther film succeeded another. Everyone knew, more or less, what Sellers was going to say because it was in the script. What was totally unpredictable was how he would say it.

They came to the scene where Sellers informs Sanders that his (Sanders') servant has been the victim of an assault. He has been found unconscious with a bump on his head. It was with the word 'bump' that Sellers reached the peak of Clouseau's linguistic Everest. A phonetican could probably use his funny symbols to render the pronunciation accurately but then only other phoneticians could read it. The best I can do is report as I remember it the exchange between Clouseau and Sanders. It went something like this.

Clouseau: Your servang as bin farnd in ze gardang. E as a bermp on is ead.

Sanders: A bermp?

Clouseau: Yes, a bermp.

Evidently this took Sanders off guard. Determined not to lose a fiver his handsome features remained as rigidly unsmiling as ever. But a tear rolled down his cheek. He had to pay.

Buster Keaton and Fatty Arbuckle used to plan enormously elaborate practical jokes which they performed with all the skill and timing that is to be seen in their films. In *Keaton: The Man Who Wouldn't Lie Down* Tom Dardis describes a Hollywood dinner given by Arbuckle in honour of Adolph Zukor, his new employer at Paramount. The joke was to be played by Keaton, and Zukor was to be the victim. All the other guests, who included Bebe Daniels and Alice Lake, had been forewarned. The idea was that Keaton should pose for the evening as a butler of unbelievable ineptitude, maladroitness and stupidity. The lights were kept low so that Zukor should not recognise Buster, a risk that was reduced by the fact that at the time (about 1919) Buster had not yet made a full-length feature film. Arbuckle's role was that of a host, who would be at first embarrassed, but finally reach a state of sheer undiluted rage.

Buster started with the hors d'oeuvre, which consisted of shrimps. He served these quite adequately, apart from the fact that he served the men before the women. Arbuckle rebuked him in no uncertain terms. 'You numbskull, don't you know better than to serve the men first?' An apologetic Buster removed the shrimps (some of which had been eaten by now) from the men and gave them to the women.

Next came soup. Buster put a plate in front of each diner and then went into the kitchen. The sound of a tremendous crash was heard, followed by various other noises of banging, breaking and tinkling. Buster then poured some kitchen slops over himself and returned to the table, dripping wet and (one imagines) with his features composed in their usual stony lack of expression. Without any explanation he removed the soup plates.

Meanwhile Arbuckle was talking loudly about the difficulty of finding good servants nowadays. He said the problem had got so bad that he was thinking of leaving Los Angeles. If this meant that he had to leave films, then so be it. Zukor began to be alarmed. He had only just signed Arbuckle up, and didn't want to lose his new and large star.

The lovely Bebe Daniels, who was sitting to Arbuckle's right, asked the butler if she could have some of the iced water in the jug he was carrying. Buster was visibly dazzled by Bebe Daniels' beauty. In Dardis's words: 'As if transfixed by Circe herself, Buster stared helplessly into her eyes while he slowly poured the entire contents of the pitcher into Arbuckle's lap. Screaming "Idiot! Idiot! Idiot!" Arbuckle seized Buster around the neck and attempted to drag him out of sight into the kitchen. He was forcibly restrained by the men at the table, and a cringing Buster retreated into the kitchen. Conversation was uneasily resumed, and the long wait for the food continued, with Zukor totally shaken by the way the evening was turning out.'

Then came the *pièce de resistance*. The turkey. This was a twenty-pounder, which Buster bore proudly through the swing doors on a silver dish, at the same time, dropping his napkin. While he was bending down to pick it up, an accomplice suddenly opened the swing door behind him, sending Buster and turkey flying. One can imagine, from having watched Keaton films, the agility with which he staged the business of attempting to retrieve the turkey, while it kept slipping from his hands and back onto the floor. But unlike a cinema audience no one laughed. The guests knew their part, and watched the performance in a beautifully acted imitation of a horrified and embarrassed silence.

Finally Buster, now well covered in gravy, managed to get the turkey back on the plate. He then started cleaning the bird with his napkin, which was by now filthy. Arbuckle went berserk. Throwing off restraining arms he chased Buster into the kitchen, whence came sounds of crashing, screams for mercy and general mayhem. This was followed by the sight from the window of Arbuckle chasing Keaton round and round the house.

Finally Arbuckle returned and announced that fortunately he had a second turkey, which would be ready in an hour or so. While this was being cooked Buster went upstairs, changed into his normal clothes and then used the house telephone to ring Arbuckle, announcing himself as Buster Keaton. Arbuckle was delighted to hear from his old friend and asked him if he would like to drop by for dessert and coffee. Keaton accepted the invitation and after a suitable interval knocked on the door. He was welcomed in and introduced to Zukor, who evidently did not recognise the butler who had earlier caused such pandemonium. It was only after pointed comments about the physical resemblance between the two men that Zukor finally tumbled.

C.O. loved this one for its qualities of slapstick. After he'd related it to me, he went on to tell of an American actor (he wouldn't, for some reason, reveal his identity) who had the misfortune to have a glass eye. Or, rather, several glass eyes of varying colours, including a bloodshot one for when he was suffering from a hangover. The actor was, it seems, a practical joker with a particularly surreal sense of humour. In restaurants he was given to studying the menu minutely, while the waiter hovered and others at the table waited for him to choose his meal. When he was assured of their attention, he would absent-mindedly scratch his eye with his fork.

As C.O. pointed out, one of the great virtues of a practical joke perpetrated on-stage is that the joke's audience is, as it were, already provided and the victim's embarrassment immediate. He told me once of a young French actor who was fortunate enough to land a leading romantic role. The part required of him that he wore a natty little moustache – provided, since the young man preferred to remain clean-shaven, by the wardrobe department. On the first night, just as he was about to go on stage, another actor, Henry Monnier, stopped him in a concerned way to point out that one half of his moustache had come off. There were only seconds to go and it would obviously be better to have no moustache at all than half a moustache. Accordingly Monnier removed one half of his colleague's moustache. The young actor made his entrance and brought the house down.

Another of Monnier's tricks was at the expense of an actor in a costume drama who was playing the part of a courtier about to present himself to the King. Monnier gently placed a hat on the courtier's big eighteenth-century wig. On his entry the actor playing the King whispered 'You fool, raise your hat.' The actor, who of course also had a hat in his hand, was very confused but did as his monarch ordered – placing one hat on top of the other. The house was brought down once more.

One of the better examples of the C.O. 'boomerang' principle was given by that great old pro, the late A.E. Matthews, who had the reputation of being completely unthrowable. Other players would go to great lengths to discountenance him, but he never fell victim to their plots. He was once playing in a drawing-room comedy when the stage telephone began to ring. In the course of a long run, this was something that had never before happened at this point in the play. Matty Matthews had obviously been set up. Without batting an eyelid he picked up the phone. 'Hullo,' he said. 'Yes . . . yes . . . I see.' Then he turned to one of the other actors and said ' It's for you.'

LETTERS PLAY

The Royal Shakespeare Company scored a tremendous hit in 1980 with its production of *Nicholas Nickleby*. Theatre-goers were therefore not too surprised when posters began to go up all over London advertising the forthcoming production of Dickens' *Little Dorrit*. At around the same time actors, producers and theatre designers all over the country received letters inviting their participation in the venture. The letters were all signed,'Love, Trev,' (Trevor Nunn is the joint Artistic Director of the Royal Shakespeare Company).

Nothing very odd about all this perhaps, except that the RSC logo on the posters and letter-headings had undergone a change. The Royal Shakespeare Company had turned into the Royal Dickens Company. And Trevor Nunn had not sent the letters.

Rather than saying the same thing to everyone, the hoaxer sent letters tailor-made to engage the interest of each recipient. John Barton, for example, is well known for his freely imaginative handling of the texts of Shakespeare and of Greek tragedies: when he feels like it, he does not hesitate to supplement these classics with his own dialogue. The RDC's letter to John Barton accordingly invited him to finish Dicken's uncompleted last novel, *The Mystery of Edwin Drood*.

Michael Bogdanov, whose nick-name is Bodge, was

asked to direct Dickens' *Sketches by Boz*. The letter to Norman St John-Stevas, then Minister for the Arts, was wonderfully straightfaced.

Dear Minister

As you have probably heard there has been a major change of policy in our organisation.

Nicholas Nickleby has been such a real joy to cast, staff and audience that we have decided to turn to Dickens as our main source of inspiration.

As someone said at a recent meeting, why tie down so many fine Dickensian directors and actors to this endless wheel of Shakespeare revivals?

I am convinced that Dickens will prove as big a draw as Shakespeare, if we can keep up this terrific standard.

So that'll be it for the bard as soon as our present commitments decently permit.

The first production of the new RDC is hoped to be *Little Dorrit*, adapted by Snoo Wilson and directed by John Caird and myself. Any thought you have on this will, as always, be treasured.

Love,
Trev

P.S. Perhaps we could get together for lunch some time. The Pickwick Club would seem appropriate!

'It is now deeply embarrassing,' Trevor Nunn told *The Times* (31 July 1980). 'A lot of people have written to me refusing, or, even more embarrassing, accepting the offers.'

The practical joker (who was in fact the avant-garde theatre director Ken Cambell) made a graceful apology. He sent Trevor Nunn copies of the letters accompanied by a quotation from Shakespeare's *The Tempest:*

> As you from crimes would pardon'd be
> Let your indulgence set me free.

Most of the famous English public schools were founded in the nineteenth century. As far as I know there has only been one notable addition to their number since the war. This was in 1948 and it was almost single-handedly the work of one Cambridge undergraduate. His name was Humphry Berkeley, later to become an MP. The school was called Selhurst, and the Headmaster's name was H. Rochester Sneath.

Selhurst was a brilliantly chosen name. It has an instant plausibility about it. Berkeley has recorded the great care with which he established that it was as convincing as he thought it to be. Over a period of months he would seize every opportunity to steer conversations with fellow under-graduates in a direction where he would be asked where he went to school. He would then reply modestly, 'Well as a matter of fact I went to a school called Selhurst.'

Registering his questioner's blank non-recognition of the name he would follow up with 'Haven't you heard of Selhurst?' Anxious not to cause offence his acquaintance would reply 'Of course I've heard of it my dear fellow.' After various such successful experiments Berkeley knew that he had found the perfect name for what he calls a minor public school of 'the third degree'.

The next move was to have some letter headings printed with words at the top reading 'Selhurst School, Near Petworth, Sussex. From The Headmaster, H. Rochester Sneath.' At small expense, but with considerable ingenuity, Berkeley was able to make a forwarding arrangement with the Post Office. (Another ruse was to pretend that he was staying on holiday with an imaginary sister to whom letters should be sent.) Now he was in business.

The first letter was to the Master of Marlborough

College. H. Rochester Sneath announced that the three-hundredth anniversary of the foundation of Selhurst was coming up, and that he was anxious to have the opportunity of entertaining Their Majesties on the occasion. 'Perhaps you would be kind enough to let me know how you managed to engineer a visit recently from the King and Queen.' He also asked for any helpful tips about how to treat royalty.

Berkeley must have been delighted to receive the Master of Marlborough's reply which was predictably, and wonderfully frosty. 'I did nothing whatever to engineer the recent royal visit.'

Unperturbed, Berkeley-Sneath wrote a letter 'in the strictest confidence' about a Mr Robert Agincourt who taught French at Selhurst for one term two years ago and was asking for a reference in support of his application for a post at Marlborough. Sneath says that he is quite unable to go along with this request. During the Agincourt's brief employment at Selhurst, he explains, no fewer than five boys had to be removed from the school as the result of his undesirable influence, and three matrons had nervous breakdowns. 'His practices were described by the Chairman of the County Hospital as "Hunnish".'

Sneath goes on to make comments about Agincourt's unfortunate appearance – in particular the prominent wart on his nose. He then describes the occasion on which Agincourt was observed climbing a tree in the school grounds at night, stark naked.

The Master's one-sentence reply stated that Agincourt had not applied for a job and that he (the Master) required no further information about the man. An equally off-putting reply came to Sneath's later request for advice about how to set about engaging a private detective.

After an exchange with George Bernard Shaw (who turned down an invitation on the grounds that he was too old at the age of 91¾) Sneath turned his attentions to another public school – Rugby. He wrote to the new Headmaster, Arthur fforde (a name to match that of Rochester Sneath himself). He apologised for his delay in sending congratulations on fforde's appointment as Headmaster, and did so with condescension of the most unctuous kind. 'Unfortunately, dear boy, I have been ill and unable to attend to correspondence for three months, but as an old friend of your father's (I used to fag for him at school), I felt that he would wish me to give you some advice.'

This he proceeds to do. Running a school is a complex business, he says. Senior masters have to be treated with tact. 'Remember that you are a man of the world, as

indeed I was when I became Headmaster, and you cannot expect the same broad-mindedness from men whose mental stature is inevitably circumscribed by the narrowness of the school surroundings .... Do not be taken in by the hysterical outcries against homosexuality which appear from time to time in the press. I have found that most homosexuality amongst schoolboys is harmless, and you can afford to ignore what is in most cases a purely transitory phase. Do not quote me as saying this, because although I believe it to be true, you cannot say that kind of thing to parents.' Arthur fforde replied thanking Rochester Sneath for a letter 'so closely packed with good and serviceable advice'.

Many other headmasters of distinguished public schools received such letters. The Headmaster of Charterhouse was puzzled by the jocular reminder of how he had broken a Sneath collar-bone while playing football many years ago. The formidable J.F. Roxburgh, founding Headmaster of Stowe and teacher of the young Evelyn Waugh at Lancing College, was asked for advice about the way to deal with the problem of sex education.

Roxburgh replied that 'The thing is best dealt with in as unemotional a manner as possible and without the element of mystery, hushed voices and vague allusions which so often make what a man says to a boy on these matters utterly unreal.'

Sensible advice no doubt, and of the kind that many a headmaster might give. What has the unmistakeable Roxburgh ring about it is referring to sex as 'the thing' which is surely as vague an allusion as a man could give.

On another occasion Rochester Sneath invited the distinguished architect Sir Giles Gilbert Scott to design a new House for the School. 'Above all, we wish for a building which will inspire clean and healthy thoughts and one in which it is easier to use the intellect than to slack.' Scott replied that he regretted that he was too heavily engaged with the re-building of the House of Commons to be able to begin work on such a scheme for the next twelve months.

Sneath's public school leg-pulling culminated in a letter to the *Daily Worker* which appeared on 13 April 1948. He announced that parents at Selhurst had objected to his scheme to introduce the compulsory study of Russian in the school, and that the Board of Trade would not issue permits for the importing of Russian textbooks. The letter concluded 'English is taught in every Russian school; ought we not to grasp this hand of friendship?'

This actually elicited a pompous reply (also published by the *Daily Worker*) from the Board of Trade's Chief Information Officer about the permitted import quotas of learned, scientific and technical books. Further letters came from the University of London's School of Slavonic and East European Studies. In fact there was quite a stink.

Indeed there was such a stink that it led to the unmasking of H. Rochester Sneath by diligent journalists following up the story. It also got Humphry Berkeley into very hot water. He was barred from visiting his Cambridge college for two years, a penalty which seems pretty severe by the standards of these post-Student Power days.

One of Sneath's dottiest letters was to the Headmaster of Tonbridge. It begins 'Dear Rootie, You will doubtless remember old "Tubby" Sneath – – well it will give you a helluva shock, you old bounder, because last year I took on the Headship here (Selhurst). Do you remember prophesying my early death in a South American brothel?' And so on, in a style that seems to anticipate that of *Private Eye's* 'Dear Bill,' letters.

The Headmaster of Tonbridge had a name which was nothing like Rootie. Nor could he remember anyone called 'Tubby' Sneath, or recollect ever prophesying such an exotic death for anyone. Naturally he wrote a puzzled reply, disassociating himself from Rootie or any other such character, and that was that.

Or was it? Could that name, in its way as brilliant as

Selhurst itself, have been the seed from which grew another celebrated hoaxer – Henry Root? This was the name appended to a large number of letters sent to public figures during the course of 1979 and early 1980. The results of this correspondence were turned into an immediate best-seller. The man behind Henry Root turned out to be William Donaldson, a man whose previous career was almost as remarkable as that of Henry Root. Donaldson produced *Beyond the Fringe*, the review which proved such a breakthrough in comedy in the 1960s. Donaldson's time as a pimp in Chelsea is recorded in his *Both the Ladies and the Gentlemen*, a book which I have not read, but which I am assured on good authority is extremely droll.

I have suggested that the name of Root might have come from Sneath. Perhaps his borrowings went further than that. The original idea of the letters seems to have been that of an American television comedian called Don Novello whose book *The Lazlo Letters* went straight into the *New York Times* best-seller list when it was published in 1977. These letters purported to come from one Lazlo Toth (named after the man who attacked Michelangelo's *Pietà* with a hammer). Like Root, Lazlo is extremely right-wing, and like Root he sends to public figures his advice and opinions. They both write to the Queen, and both try to get their appalling literary efforts into print. Like Root, Lazlo receives entertaining replies from his puzzled victims. The design of the Root book also bore a striking similarity to the Lazlo one. In the publicity attending the publication of the Root letters, William Donaldson acknowledged his debt to Don Novello, but did not do so in the book. Well, well. Shakespeare wrote about Falstaff before Verdi did, and they both made a good job of it.

ART OF HOAX AND HOAX OF ART

The Arts Council of Great Britain is an organisation with which C.O. had an odd love-hate relationship. Rumour has it that he was a member of the Literature Panel for two years – posing, of course, as someone else, someone whose letter politely declining the position had been intercepted by C.O. It's not clear quite how C.O. made 'practical' use of his status as a mole, though anyone following the activities backed by some of the panels and sub-committees might have discovered one or two instances of C.O.'s handiwork.

The Arts Council has certainly financed some pretty dotty things (and, in fairness, some dotty pretty things). The notorious pile of bricks at the Tate is nothing to some of the things the Arts Council has supported. So much so that there seemed no particular reason to disbelieve the press release on Arts Council paper that in January 1981 drew attention to a 'cityscape sculpture' called 'Dead Shore', the work of Arthur Styles RA. This turned out to be an exceptionally ugly piece of scaffolding shoring up two houses in Ledbury Road, Notting Hill.

The art world can take this kind of thing lying down (or in any other position). Not so, apparently, the local population who sent a shoal of protesting letters to the local rag, the *Kensington Post*, denouncing this so-called neo-constructivist work of art. The *Kensington Post* was all set for an article on the subject, but discovered in time that none of the names of the letter-writers was to be found in the telephone book. Nor had the Royal Academy heard of Arthur Styles. Nor had the Arts Council heard of his masterpiece 'Dead Shores'.

Modern art might appear to be a sitting duck, but in fact it can fire back. In 1917 Marcel Duchamp helped assemble the Society of Independent Artists' exhibition in New York. Theoretically there was no selection committee, the show being open to any artist who paid a six-dollar fee. Nevertheless Duchamp's work was rejected. It consisted of a porcelain urinal which he signed with the fictitious name of R. Mutt.

Duchamp stoutly defended R. Mutt's work. Indeed he based on it a creed which was to have great importance for the future of art, and indeed poetry. 'Whether Mr Mutt with his own hands made the fountain or not has no importance,' he wrote. 'He *chose* it. He took an ordinary article of life, placed it so that its useful significance disappeared under a new title and point of view – Mr Mutt created a new thought for that object.'

Since then there have been many occasions when it has been hard to know when an artist is playing a joke on the public, and when a practical joke is being played on the art world. (The same is true of modern music, where there have been some notable hoaxes indistinguishable from some of the stuff that can be heard in concert halls and on Radio 3.)

Take, as example, the German impressionist painter from Lubeck, Bruno Hat. C.O.'s records tell us that on 23 June 1929 an exhibition of his work opened at the Buckingham Street house of Brian Guinness (later Lord Moyne). The paintings varied in style from cubism to surrealism. Some were plain canvases with bits of cork and wool stuck to them. The catalogue's explanatory essay, 'Approach to Hat', was the usual highfalutin critical waffle.

Hat was there in person. According to Tom Driberg, the

artist 'sat in a wheelchair, a morose, taciturn figure with a marked German accent, a moustache worthy of Harry Tate, and smoked glasses.' When an art-lover admired a painting framed in rope, Hat replied, 'Ja, it ees mine own idea.' Lady Diana Mosley thought the pictures 'lovely'. Lytton Strachey actually bought one.

Only after the art critics had written up the show with enthusiasm did the *Daily Express* run the headline 'Amazing Hoax on Art Experts – Unknown Artist with False Moustache – Mr Bruno Hat.' It turned out that the person of Bruno Hat was in fact Tom Mitford, the catalogue introduction was by Evelyn Waugh and the whole jape had been thought up by Brian Howard.

This joke proved to be a particularly long-lived one, for Bruno Hat's painting 'Pears in a Bowl' came up for sale at Christie's in October 1980. It was signed 'Bruno', dated 1929 and was in fact (the Christie's catalogue explained) the work of John Banting, a close friend of Brian Howard's. It fetched £500. I must say I thought it was rather good.

That's the trouble with spoofs on the arts. They do tend to be rather good. So much knowledge, ability and

Actually, it's a *Canard*... but it's a very good one

inventiveness is needed to produce a passable spoof, hoax or fraud that more often than not real quality creeps in (as it does in good parody). This is certainly true of the famous literary frauds, such as Macpherson's Ossian or Chatterton's supposed discoveries or the works of Ern Malley.

James McNeil Whistler was the hero of another of C.O.'s artist stories. On a visit to Venice Whistler noticed a fellow artist in the Piazza San Marco who was painting a picture in which every detail, every stone, every brick was painstakingly and minutely, recorded. Whistler's own paintings tended to be on the foggy side, and were very different from this kind of Royal Academy stuff.

Whistler took a board and wrote on it, in several languages, the words COMPLETELY BLIND. He propped this up behind the painter who was much perplexed by the admiring crowd that soon gathered around him and started dropping coins into the hat which Whistler had also thoughtfully provided.

Among C.O. Jones's more recent press-cuttings was a front page of the Glasgow *Evening Times* for 22 August 1980, which carried a hot story under the headline 'Top Pole Flees To Safety'. C.O.'s accompanying note, paper-clipped to the cutting, reminded me that this was during the earliest days of the Solidarity movement and obviously a news story of the greatest possible interest both in human and political terms. Ian Buchan's 'exclusive' report told how the dissident Polish artist Anton Krashny was fleeing from house arrest in order to attend the Edinburgh Festival. There, Buchan was able to reveal, Krashny would be guest of honour at a dinner attended also by the Festival's Director, John Drummond, by the broadcaster Joan Bakewell, and by the cartoonist Emilio Coia. Krashny was going to take this opportunity to ask for political asylum and to make an impassioned plea to the Polish authorities to come to terms with the Solidarity strikers.

Buchan had evidently worked hard on the story, for he had even managed to track down and interview Krashny's daughter Rebecca, then living in Edinburgh. 'Thank God,' was her reaction to the news of her father's impending arrival. 'I was beginning to think I'd never see him again.' She spoke of her artist father's life as a painter in Scotland, New Mexico and Bolivia, and revealed that Anton Krashny had another family in Poland, including triplets.

Readers of the Glasgow *Evening Times* must have been puzzled when in the next days the paper not only failed to follow up this interesting story but didn't even mention it. The reason, which was not explained to them, was simple. The unfortunate reporter had been hoaxed.

Anton Krashny didn't exist, except in the imaginations of various people who had been at an Edinburgh Festival party some years previously. They had there invented the Polish dissident artist in what is frankly admitted to have been a drunken moment. Prime movers were Joan Bakewell and Clark Tait, a Scottish Television producer. 'Rebecca' was in fact Rebecca Irvine, who was working at the time at the Edinburgh Festival office. It seems to have been sheer bad luck that she should have been the person to answer the phone when Buchan rang up to check on the story.

Joan Bakewell told all to Peter Dunn (*The Sunday Times*, 7 September 1980). She confessed that 'Anton Krashny' was 'floated on a tide of alcohol and Edinburgh euphoria' some five years previously, when she was making a documentary about the Festival. From that point he had taken on a life of his own 'decked out with all sorts of nonsense'. At the Edinburgh Festival there is an annual Krashny dinner, at which The Scrotum is piped in on a silver platter. There's a Krashny Society with Clark Tait as Life President, Douglas Rae (a reporter from Scottish Television) as Chairman, and Joan Bakewell as Lady President.

It was Douglas Rae who fed the wretched Buchan the original tale of the defecting Krashny. Relations between

Scottish Television and the Glasgow *Evening Times* had been not too rosy for some time. They were not exactly improved as a result of the Krashny affair. A tight-lipped spokesman for the *Evening Times* would only say that 'certain people aren't being bought whiskies at the bar any more,' – no mean threat in Scotland.

The story had a bizarre sequel. A few months later Joan Bakewell received information through the post about an impending exhibition at London's Francis Kyle gallery of a collection of prints by Anton Krajnc, an Austrian-born lithographer. Anton Krajnc? Anton Krashny? Miss Bakewell understandably assumed that the joke had boomeranged and that this time it was she who was being set up as the fall-person. On investigation it turned out that there really was an Anton Krajnc and that he really was having an exhibition of prints in London; an example, as C.O.'s annotations suggest, of life limping lamely along in the wake of the art of practical joking. Joan Bakewell was quoted as saying that she was thinking seriously of buying one of his prints. I hope she did. It might have cheered her up when not being bought whiskies by the staff of the Glasgow *Evening Times*.

Although C.O. Jones was a great exponent of the 'practical' element in practical joking (a man ill-organised in his private life, he was always able to bring a high degree of order to his japes), he also admired wit. Perhaps it was this, together with his own use of paint and canvas for the

'Sacré Coeur' joke, that caused him to so admire Alphonse Allais (1854-1905), a man whom Miles Kington describes as probably the finest humorous writer France has ever produced: a judgement with which (apart from a querying rumour about whether Rabelais was a humourist) it is hard to quarrel.

Allais was a writer first and foremost, and much of his writing contains a practical joke element that he seems to have carried into real life too (and back again). However, one of C.O.'s favourite Allais stories concerned an art exhibition held by Allais and some of his Bohemian friends. The joke lay in the fact that none of the exhibitors could draw. They weren't just bad artists, you understand, but people who *genuinely* had no talent at all. The show was called the Salon des Incoherents. Allais's own contribution gives him a claim to be the first man ever to paint an entirely abstract picture. It was a large canvas, entirely black, entitled 'Negroes Fighting in a Cave at Night'. This proved such a success that Allais followed it with six more canvases on similar lines. These included the all-white 'Anaemic Young Girls Going to Their First Communion through a Blizzard', an all-red one called 'Apoplectic Cardinals Harvesting Tomatoes by the Red Sea', and an all-blue one called 'Stupefied Naval Cadets Seeing the Mediterranean for the First Time'.

Allais' achievements were many and various. If anything his athletic achievements were even more remarkable than his literary ones. For example, he held the world record for free-style cycling over one millimetre, having covered the distance in 1/17,000 of a second without the aid of pacemakers. I have checked with the *Guinness Book of Records*, and as far as I can see this record has never been beaten.

Allais was also a considerable inventor. His inventions included water-proof curtains for submarines, a luminous hat for wearing at night, a power-assisted horse, a bus without brakes, a combined fishing-rod and bicycle pump, a self-locking saucer, a bullet-proof haversack, a combined saltcellar/cigar-holder, and a device to keep the body upright during long train journeys. How sad that no enterprising entrepreneur was prepared to back these ideas with money and exploit them properly.

One of Allais' constant victims was a distinguished drama critic of the day called Francisque Sarcey. In his magazine *Chat Noir* Allais used to write parodies of Sarcey, often actually signing them with Sarcey's name. Sometimes he would even appear in public pretending to be Sarcey. On one such occasion, Allais invited a young man to dinner with him the next night and gave Sarcey's real address, at the same time warning the admirer that he (Sarcey) had a younger brother who was under the delusion that *he* was the real drama critic. If his brother happened to be there (and he usually was, as he was kept at home on account of his unfortunate tendency to molest children) the guest should be sure to treat him sternly and tell him, 'I know all about you and those young kids!'

The young man turned up, duly refused to believe that his host was the drama critic, and made pointed comments about his unusual interest in children. When Sarcey (the real Sarcey) insisted that he *was* Sarcey, the young man blandly remarked that in that case he had changed a great deal since their meeting at the *Chat Noir* the previous evening. At this point Sarcey detected Allais's hand at work. He took the joke in good part, and insisted that the young man should stay for dinner.

Allais was highly proprietorial about Sarcey. When another writer published a Sarcey parody, Allais wrote a furious letter to the journal in which it appeared. In denouncing the impostor, Allais wrote: 'There are only two men in Paris entitled to sign themselves Francisque Sarcey. Firstly me, and secondly, Francisque Sarcey.'

One of Allais' stories (and it is often hard to tell whether they are really true or whether he thought them up and dashed them off over a glass of absinthe when he had a deadline to catch) concerned his friend Leon Dumachin. While Dumachin was on his honeymoon in Munich he found that his announcement that they were about to visit Kleinsberg was greeted with laughter by a German friend. The explanation was that the Three Kings Hotel, the only respectable place to stay in Kleinsberg, had a standard trick which was played on honeymoon couples. In the young married people's room a piece of string was tied inconspicuously to the head of the bed, and went through a hole in the floor to the bar below. At the end of the string was a cork. Any movement of the bed set the cork dancing, to the simple amusement of the drinking classes of Kleinsberg.

On arrival at the Three Kings, Dumachin found everything to be as predicted. To the puzzlement of his wife (who hadn't been let in on the story) he got on the floor with scissors and travelling clock. So as not to arouse suspicion downstairs, he made sure not to twitch the string as he cut it free. He then tied the string to the minute-hand of the clock.

'Can you picture the scene?' Allais wrote. 'All those good people downstairs, smoking their pipes and supping from their tankards, sitting all evening watching the cork go slowly, slowly up and slowly, slowly down again. I have no idea what went through their German minds. But I am told that by six o'clock in the morning half Kleinsberg was in the bar with their eyes fixed on the all-revealing cork. I'm afraid they must have thought that the reputation of the French as great lovers was somewhat exaggerated.'

A similar trick was attributed to Abraham Lincoln, a fact which perhaps throws a different light on that austere bearded countenance. But then it was Lincoln who, as a young man, painted a room and, while the paint was still wet, took a pair of shoes and made footprints that walked up one wall, across the ceiling, and down to the floor again.

There is a sense in which any representational painting is

a practical joke. The artist uses his skill to make you think you are looking at a bowl of apples, or the Princess of Wales, or Clapham Common, or whatever, when in fact you are looking at an arrangement of variously coloured pigments spread thinly on stretched canvas or primed hardboard. The artist is an illusionist, which is doubtless why C.O. chose to study art after he left Borstal (I hadn't mentioned that, had I? But then he rarely mentioned it himself, beyond occasional references to his 'initial period of further education after leaving school'.)

C.O.'s career as a painter was, frankly, not successful. He disliked the restrictions of the conventional framed rectangle which the galleries favour. He preferred to exercise his skills by executing such works as the extremely realistic door-handle he painted on my bathroom door, or the coat-hook in the hall. Bathroom and hall are both dimly lit and visitors are still regularly taken in by the illusions C.O. created. He even perpetrated such deceptions of his own person: hating the chore of polishing his shoes he would often *paint* them to the required colour, complete with subtle highlights suggesting a gloss normally acquired only by much polish and elbow-grease.

He had quite a collection of examples of practical jokes concerning artists, and was probably working on this subject when I last saw him. At any rate, that particular file seems to be missing. I remember, though, his story about Gustave Courbet. Champfleury, a friend of the painter's, once noticed in Courbet's studio a package addressed to a Russian Princess. Champfleury slipped into the package a note saying 'Madame, I love you with all my heart.' Courbet was understandably surprised when a few days later the Princess turned up bearing the note. Courbet truthfully denied having written the note. When the Princess asked if he recognised the writing he stood on his dignity and stated that he was an artist, not an expert on handwriting . . . That seemed to be the end of the matter. It wasn't.

The years passed and Courbet forgot all about the incident, the joker remaining undiscovered. Then one day the Princess, now advanced in years, turned up at his studio again. 'Monsieur Courbet,' she said 'I always knew you were a gallant man. No, don't deny it. Do you think I ever doubted that it was really you who sent me that note. No, there's no longer any need to protest. Don't worry. The Prince is dead. I am free. I am yours.'

MENCKEN ABOUT

It was one of C.O.'s most strongly held theories that practical joking is in the blood. Somewhere, he claimed, in the make-up of the inveterate practical joker, there must lie an errant gene – a tiny biological quirk that provides both the inventiveness necessary to devise the joke and the ability to enjoy its outcome. He was invariably secretive about his antecedents, so I was never able to tell whether he believed his own particular talent to have been inherited from his mother or his father. On one occasion, though, he did let slip a tiny clue when he made reference to his father's 'temporary absences from home'; I also seem to recall him mentioning, once, that his mother suffered from 'bouts of nervous prostration'.

At any rate, it seems significant that C.O. often expressed an admiration for the Menckens, *père et fils*, and instanced them as proof of his genetic theory. H. L. Mencken, the better known of the two, was an American literary critic and journalist. His father ran a cigar manufacturing business in Baltimore. It appears that the business brought in a satisfying quantity of money and, since most of the work was done by other people, was not too arduous. He was therefore able to spend a good deal of time in the saloon next to his office, which he preferred to other saloons not only because of its proximity but also on account of the credulity of Ehoff, the old German proprietor. Mencken *père* would solemnly complain to Ehoff that his ice was stale, or tell him that the Brooklyn Bridge had fallen down, or that Bismarck was moving to Baltimore with the intention of opening a brewery.

When he and his brother had nothing better to do, which seems to have been quite often, they would pass the time thinking up what the younger Mencken called 'hoaxes and *canards*'. The one they were most proud of was the creation of a mythical brother Fred, who was supposed to be a clergyman. Since *their* father (H.L.'s grandfather) was a notorious non-believer, they put it about that Fred was considered a disgrace to the family. This was why Fred's presence was, so to speak, conspicuous by its absence. Visitors were warned that on no account should Fred be mentioned, for fear of upsetting the old man. Nor should the clergy be mentioned when he was in the room, 'lest his sorrow suddenly overwhelm and unman him'.

Over the years the Fred legend was developed in elaborate detail. Fred had been invited to become chaplain of the United States Senate. Fred had made more than 5,000 converts in a single week in Chicago. Finally his brothers made Fred a bishop and left it at that. In his autobiographical *Happy Days* H.L. Mencken says that half a century later he would still sometimes be stopped by a rheumy old Baltimorean asking him what became of his uncle Fred.

Another story involved a dilapidated summer home that Mencken's *père* bought in Mount Washington. One of his new neighbours asked, casually, if he had plans for developing the place. He solemnly replied that he intended to use the front lawn for breeding 'blooded hogs, a race too much neglected in Maryland'. This alarming story spread quickly, but he still had time to greet the first protest delegation with large blueprints of the proposed piggery. These plans had been drawn up by a builder friend and clearly showed the name 'Pig Hill' strung on a large banner from two vast flagpoles at the main entrance to the property. As time went by and nothing happened, the excitement began to die down, but the name 'Pig Hill' stuck, and was gradually extended to the whole settlement.

H.L. Mencken admits some of his father's 'solo flights' – presumably meaning the hoaxes carried out without his brother's assistance – were 'perilously close to the line limiting the best of taste'. In fact he actually uses the word 'barbarity' about a trick on a totally inoffensive German friend who owned a wood-working factory and whose only known indulgence was an occasional game of cards with a few friends. When this harmless old man found himself involved in a business law-suit he became worried that news of it might reach the ears of Bradstreet's, the commercial credit agency, thereby inducing them to reduce his credit rating. Mencken Senior obligingly offered to apply for a Bradstreet report on him to ascertain whether this had actually happened. He then made out a bogus Bradstreet report which comprehensively rubbished the wretched woodworker, accusing him of hanging around with suspicious characters, drinking heavily, and squandering his money at the card table. The report concluded by hinting that his family was thinking of having him put away as being *non compos mentis*, and that his creditors were planning to put him into liquidation.

The old man's reaction was understandably extreme. 'He leaped in the air, began God-damning horribly in English and German, and talked wildly of shaking the dust of the United States from his feet and going back to his native Bremen.' He was soon so violently worked up that Mencken rapidly confessed, but the victim was too overwrought to listen. Only the acquisition of a genuine Bradstreet's report (highly complimentary) was able to calm the old man down.

The elder Mencken had plenty of time and money to spend on his hoaxes. He was also not exactly left-wing. In his later years he would unrepentantly reminisce about what he considered the true peak of his talent. This was his successful wrecking of the cigarmakers' union of Baltimore, which called a strike there in about 1889. The union's funds were too small to pay out full benefits. The best it could do was to provide free tickets to Philadelphia, which at that time had so many cigar shops that it was known as the Cigarmaker's Heaven. This offer was also open to non-union freelance cigarmakers: the union was eager to clear out these casuals, who were usually half-starved and could easily be induced by the bosses to act as strike-breakers.

All that the union required as credentials was the possession of the tools of the trade – a boxwood cutting-board and cutting tools. What Mencken did was to acquire quantities of this equipment. He then had a number of drunks and tramps rounded up, gave them a drink, fifty cents, cutting board and tools, the address of the union headquarters and instructions on what to say when they got there. He claimed that in the course of a few weeks 'at least a thousand poor bums were run through the mill' at a cost to the union of $2.10 a head. When it was clear that the union was all but wrecked, the brute delivered his *coup de grâce*. This was achieved by rounding up a dozen *one-armed* men, and marching them off to the union headquarters. Since cigar-making is evidently a two-handed job, the hoax was exposed, but by then the union had no money left. The strike was broken, and the cigarmakers' union was not heard of again in Baltimore for many years. One can understand why the chapter on practical jokes in *Happy Days* is frankly titled 'Recreations of a Reactionary'.

C.O. Jones considered, or so he told me, that the elder Mencken's strike-breaking joke was quite definitely over the top; even so, he clearly admired the ability to organise and the sheer dedication that had gone into it. That was one of C.O.'s invariable ingredients for a really successful joke – dedication, thoroughness, an ability to *convince*. The Menckens certainly possessed that quality. C.O. would provide evidence of the fact by pointing to a joke played by H.L. Mencken which was so effective as to survive its perpetrator's confession. C.O. loved those – the ones that were actually exposed as jokes, but continued, nonetheless, to be taken seriously. He was overjoyed, for instance, to hear of the invention, in America, of an organisation called 'The League for Animal Decency'. The League declared itself to be opposed to the unblushing acceptance by most people of the flagrant displaying of animals' private parts. It campaigned, it complained, its leaders preached violently against this laxity in morals. It was given press-space and air-time; and before long, its converts were equipping their dogs with breeches, their cows with bras, their horses with cod-pieces. One farmer even went so far as to paint out his prize bull's ganglia. And long after the League's leaders had announced the organisation to be a practical joke, it continued to attract members who saw to it that animals all over the US were parading the streets, or cropping the fields, dressed in an assortment of brightly coloured underwear.

But on to H.L. Mencken's joke-that-wouldn't-lie-down. As everyone knows, our ancestors were filthy. After an admirably clean start by the Romans, who would build a bath at the drop of whatever Romans wore on their heads, cleanliness was replaced by godliness. Indeed, so far apart did the two become that baths became almost synonymous with brothels. But the idea of washing did not go entirely out of fashion. Queen Elizabeth, it is said, had a bath once a month whether she was dirty or not.

The great clean-up was slow in coming, the new-fangled private bath-tub being approached with extreme caution. As with most important innovations, the United States lagged behind. In his authoritative work on typhus, *Rats, Lice and History*, Hans Zinsser writes: 'Baths were therapeutic procedures not to be recklessly prescribed after October. The first bath-tubs did not reach America . . . we believe . . . until about 1840.' It's lucky for him that he put 'we believe' in because Zinsser appears to have been yet another victim of a hoax that went out of control and seems destined to run and run. It happened like this.

On 26 December 1917 H.L. Mencken wrote an article in the New York *Evening Mail* under the title of 'A Forgotten Anniversary'. This was about the introduction of the first bath-tub to the United States, which Mencken said, was done on 10 December 1842 by Adam Thompson of Cincinnati, who got the idea from Lord John Russell on a trip to England some ten years earlier. Thompson's bath was made of ivory lined with lead, and he inaugurated it during the course of a stag party. Thompson was surprised and disappointed by the hostile reception that greeted his innovation. Doctors denounced it as a threat to health. In Boston a municipal decree forbade its use except on medical advice. The State of Virginia slapped a $30 tax on every new bath installed, and many large towns imposed an extra charge for the additional water used in baths. Philadelphia planned to issue a decree forbidding the use of baths between November and May, but the bill failed to get a majority. Gradually, however, the bath made headway in the face of hostile officialdom and medical opinion. The imprimatur of respectability came when Millard Fillmore, President of the United States from 1850-53, had a bath installed in the White House.

Such was Mencken's narrative. Needless to say he had made the whole thing up as a practical joke. As he later explained, he was simply having a bit of Christmas-time fun as a relief from the daily battering of war-time reporting, imagining that the whole thing would be forgotten in a few days. He was wrong. It ran and ran. In 1926 he wrote a long article entitled 'Melancholy Reflections' which was syndicated in thirty American newspapers. He confessed everything and went on to tell how in the nearly ten years that had passed since he wrote the spoof article he had repeatedly come across the bogus facts coming from the pens of other writers. Quack doctors were using his 'facts' to demonstrate the stupidity of the medical profession. The medical profession was using them as examples of the progress in public hygiene. They had been quoted in scientific journals. They had been quoted in Congress. They had crossed the Atlantic and been solemnly discussed. Mencken had even come across them in reference books.

His attempt to nail the story was completely unsuccessful. As we have seen, Zinsser was saying in 1935 that bath-tubs reached America in about 1840. But Zinsser was not the only one to believe the story. Adam Thompson and his fight to have the bath-tub accepted in American society had become fact, whatever Mencken might say. Only months after his confession, *Scribner's* (October 1926) ran an article on 'The First American Bath-tub' which repeated Mencken's entire fabrication. In the year 1931 alone articles on the early history of American baths appeared in *Puritan's Progress*, the *New York Sun*, the *New York Herald Tribune*, the Baltimore *Evening Sun* (which actually employed Mencken), the Tucson *Daily Star* and the *Military Review*. Other distinguished journals that have repeated the story have included the *New Yorker* and the *New Statesman*. Some journals even illustrated the articles with illustrations of Adam Thompson being arrested in the act of taking a bath. Joseph Nathan Kane's 1933 book on 757 great American inventions includes the whole Mencken story.

In 1952 President Truman gave a speech in Philadelphia about the great progress made in the area of public health in America. By way of an example of how much better things had got (or, as he would doubtless have said, gotten) he came out with the whole Adam Thompson story. Truman gave especial credit to his predecessor President Millard Fillmore, and emphasised the importance of his initiative in putting a bath in the White House.

Doubtless there are, and long will be, further examples of people treating the tale of Adam Thompson as fact. At the end of *El Cid* the voice-over told us that Charlton Heston was riding out of the pages of history and into legend. Adam Thompson's fate has been the opposite.

SCIENTIFICALLY SPEAKING

Experts in general, and scientific experts in particular, are wonderfully gullible, and some of the best hoaxes have been at their expense. The skull of Piltdown Man is an obvious example and considered by C.O. to be one of the great classics. More recently we have had the entertaining case of various benders of spoons who had little difficulty in taking in the Professors of this and that – and under laboratory conditions too. They've been much less successful at duping professional conjurors and sceptical laymen who may not have known how the trick was done, but nonetheless did not jump to the conclusion that the metal-twisters had para-normal powers.

Observation is – or should be – of paramount importance to the scientist. This was a point constantly reiterated by Dr Joseph Bell, the eminent Edinburgh surgeon who is said to have given the idea of Sherlock Holmes to Conan Doyle, who studied medicine under him.

In the words of the *Dictionary of National Biography*, 'It was Bell's custom to impress upon his pupils the value in diagnosis of close observation of facts and the intelligent interpretation of them.' C.O. Jones used to tell the following story about Dr. Bell.

Bell was addressing his medical students and was as usual emphasising the importance of close observation and intelligent interpretation. He gave a practical example. Producing a sample of urine, he dipped his finger in and then tasted. He then told his students to do the same. Some felt a certain reluctance, even repugnance, but in the line of duty overcame their feelings and followed Bell's example. They dipped, they hesitated, they tasted.

'Now,' said Bell, 'what can we learn from this little experiment? What can we observe?'

Various students made what they hoped were intelligent observations about the colour, taste and smell of the urine. These comments were doubtless perfectly accurate but, in the word of Bell's fictional counterpart, elementary. Not one of them, Bell announced, had succeeded in observing the really important thing. This was that he had dipped his index finger in the urine.

What, the students wondered, was so important about that?

Nothing in itself, Bell replied. But they had also failed to observe that he had tasted his middle finger.

C.O.'s files record another such story of scientific gullibility. About twenty years ago the President of the Canadian Medical Association was addressing a medical convention. He intended to give a spoof lecture on the circulation of blood. Equipped with bogus X-rays, cardiographs and so on, he described a newly-observed clinical syndrome.

In measuring blood pressure there is a diastolic (low) level and a systolic (high) level on each heart beat. The Association's President described cases in which the low level became so high that it was higher than the high level, thereby causing the whole system to go into reverse, with the blood flowing in the direction opposite to normal.

Naturally he assumed that his medical audience would twig after the first few minutes. Instead he was listened to respectfully, and completed the lecture without a titter. Afterwards various distinguished quacks said they had come across the same condition.

It was, I recall, a rainy evening in London when C.O. Jones told me of one of the best instances of a practical joke that had its conclusion in severely practical usage. The rain had obliged us to seek refuge on licensed premises. We stood at the bar, hemmed in, or so it seemed, by juke boxes and electronic games screens. C.O. approved of this gadgetry no more than I. Why the serious business of drinking should be accompanied by caterwaulings and two-tone bleeps is beyond me. I said as much to C.O. – and reminded him of a recent practical joker named Fred O'Brien who, like C.O. and myself, was irritated by the follies of twentieth-century gadgetry. O'Brien was a graphic designer and employed his talent in pursuit of a practical joke. He sent to *Design Magazine* his plan for a sun-dial that could be used at night. It was luminous, pocket-sized and with an auxiliary light source.

Design Magazine published the thing, even though Mr O'Brien had explained that it was a spoof. It was taken up by the BBC's *Tomorrow's World*, who had spotted the hoax but suspected it to be fraud rather than humour. They phoned Mr O'Brien and asked how the thing worked. 'Photo-synthetic sound,' he replied, adding that the device was going to be manufactured in Japan. He later informed them that the Japan deal had fallen through because the angle of the sun in Japan is three and a half minutes out.

The next thing was that a London entrepreneur rang O'Brien to ask if the night-time sun-dial could be made more cheaply out of plastic. O'Brien explained that the whole thing was a joke. The entrepreneur registered this information, but said it was still a good idea, and in no time 150,000 luminous pocket sun-dials were being manufactured in Hong Kong. A bewildered Mr O'Brien, who was on 50 per cent of the profits, told the *Sunday Times* (15 March 1981) 'I could make more money from a joke that backfired than from my more serious work.'

Mr O'Brien has also invented an electric tea-towel bearing the words DO NOT GET WET. There's no record, though, of any manufacturer taking *that* up.

WAR GAMES

The British Army defines a booby-trap as 'a practical joke with permanent effects'. Not only is the definition chillingly accurate but it also reminds one of just how large is the contribution to warfare made by practical jokes (albeit grim ones). It's not just booby-traps but also ambushes, false information used to mislead the enemy, and all the other ruses, tactics, stratagems and wiles that are so often the most effective weapons of a military commander. As Thomas Hobbes wrote in the seventeenth century, 'Force and fraud in war are the two cardinal virtues'.

The most celebrated military practical joke of antiquity was of course the one thought up by the wily Odysseus – namely, the Trojan Horse. Malcolm's ruse of disguising his army as Birnam forest when attacking Macbeth's Dunsinane Castle is another example. In modern times the best-known is probably the Man Who Never Was. The body of a man dressed in the uniform of a Major in the Royal Marines was dropped in the sea off southern Spain equipped with documents which made it appear that the Allies were about to invade Sardinia and Greece. This deception caused the Germans to divert an entire armoured division to Greece. Whereupon the Allies invaded Sicily.

I don't know who it was that provided the British Army with its booby-trap definition, but I wouldn't be at all surprised to learn that it was Professor R.V. Jones (no relation of C.O.'s). In his fascinating book *Most Secret War* Jones describes his work as Director of Scientific Intelligence during the Second World War. First of all, this involved working out what the Germans were up to, on the basis of information that came from Ultra, the ingenious Enigma code-breaking device at Bletchley Park.

Other information was gathered from aerial photographs taken by intrepid RAF pilots, and from heroic agents in the occupied territories. But some of the intelligence came from – well, Jones's intelligence.

In trying to read the minds of the enemy on the basis of tiny clues, R.V. Jones showed truly Holmes-like powers of deduction. His imagination was fuelled not only by his scientific knowledge. For example, Jones received information to the effect that the Germans were installing a device called Wotan. He already knew that they had a navigational system involving two beams used to locate a target by the conventional means of triangulation, based on the point where the two beams intersected.

What, then, was Wotan? Since he was the most important Teutonic god (also known as Odin and still remembered in the word Wednesday) it seemed an appropriate name for a

111

powerful device. What other attributes did Wotan have? Jones read up on the subject and noted that Wotan had only one eye. This slender evidence enabled Jones to deduce that the Germans had devised a navigational device using only one beam.

Having figured out what the Germans were up to – not only with Wotan but also in a host of other cases – R.V. Jones had to think up counter-measures, and means of using the information in such a way that the enemy didn't know he knew. For example, 'bending' the beams so that the Luftwaffe dropped their bombs in the wrong place.

In these counter-measures he put to serious use the skill in practical joking that he had already developed in peace-time. Jones was a pioneer of telephone practical jokes. One of these he played on a scientist colleague at Cambridge before the war. First he made several calls, each time ringing off before the phone could be answered. Having thus given the impression that there was a fault on the line, he dialled again and this time allowed the call to be answered.

Purporting to be a telephone engineer, he said that the GPO had received complaints from telephone users who had been failing to get through to his number. It might (he said) be necessary to send a telephone engineer, but it was possible that there was a simple electrical leak which (with the subscriber's co-operation) might be traced at once.

Jones first persuaded his victim to sing loudly, on the pretext that the granules in the receiver might have seized up. When the man had sung lustily into the telephone (to the surprise of other members of the household) Jones said that the microphone was now clear and they could proceed to trace the leak. He made the man go through various antics, including standing in the middle of the room on one leg, before announcing that what they wanted was a good 'earth'. It was only when the man was on the point of plunging the telephone into a bucket of water that he was physically restrained by a collaborator of Jones's who revealed the hoax, and stopped it going too far.

A colleague of Jones's at Cambridge was the German Nobel Prize-winning physicist Carl Bosch, who once worked in a laboratory overlooking a block of flats, one of which was occupied by a journalist. Bosch phoned the journalist, pretending to be his own Professor. He announced that he had just perfected a new invention which enabled the user of an ordinary telephone to be able not only to hear but also to *see* what was going on at the other end of the line. Since this was in the early 1930s when the possibility of television was in the air, the reporter was less incredulous than he might otherwise have been.

Bosch told the journalist to point his telephone receiver towards the centre of the room, where he should then stand in any position he chose – for example holding up his right hand, or crouching, or whatever. The instructions were carried out, and on the man's returning to the phone Bosch (who had a clear view through the window) gave a precise description of what the journalist had done. The newspaperman, much impressed, lost no time in writing about Bosch's Professor and his amazing invention. The excited report was published conspicuously in his newspaper the next day.

I don't know why telephone hoaxes should be so popular in Cambridge, but I well remember David Frost trying one when we were both at university in the late 1950s. The cold war was very cold in those days, and there was much talk about Civil Defence – a subject that was held up to scornful mockery a couple of years later in the Oxbridge *Beyond the Fringe* review put together by Peter Cook and Jonathan Miller (Cambridge) and Alan Bennett and Dudley Moore (Oxford).

Frost dialled a local number at random and told the lady who replied that the GPO in collaboration with the Civil Defence people was carrying out experiments with a view to delivering water by telephone in the eventuality of normal water supplies being contaminated by nuclear fallout.

He persuaded her to hold the telephone receiver over a bucket, and then made water-gurgling noises. She replied to his inquiry that no water was coming out. Frost said they were having problems because there was too much wire at his end. Could she go to the wall at the point where her telephone line began? Now could she give it a tug? He thanked her politely, saying that she had succeeded in taking up the slack. Was there any water in the bucket yet? No, she said, but she thought the receiver was definitely getting damp.

But back to R.V. Jones. His war-time work was so secret that it often had to be kept away not only from the Germans but also from his own colleagues. One of these was an inquisitive man who, in civilian life, had been an optician. In conversation someone remarked how useful it would be to have a material that was both transparent to light and was also a conductor of electricity.

The optician remarked knowledgeably that there was no such transparent material. No, said Jones, and then (after a long thoughtful pause) added, 'Well, no, not officially.'

The optician thought he had at last cottoned on to what Jone's hush-hush Group E was up to. Jones had no difficulty in persuading the optician that they were trying to develop a transparent and invisible battleship. So far, though, (he revealed) they only had enough of the material to make a transparent torpedo-boat. The trouble was that they hadn't yet found a way of hiding the ship's wake, or of making the crew invisible.

Needless to say the Germans were playing tricks on the Allies as assiduously as we were on them. Jones had an insight into one of these as a result of a peace-time joke played by the American physicist R.W. Wood, one of whose tricks involved placing a large gyroscope in full spin inside a suitcase. He would then find an excuse to ask someone to pick up the suitcase and follow him. Since it wasn't very heavy it was not hard to carry, but the porter would be extremely puzzled when he tried to turn a corner and met resistance from the gyroscopic suitcase. (Try it with a toy gyroscope in action. It's easy to pick up, hard to knock over.)

Wood didn't confine himself, though, to mechanical aids for his practical jokes. At one time, he lived in a block of flats in Paris; the lady in the flat below had a tortoise which she kept in a window-box. Wood first laid in a supply of tortoises of various sizes, and then rigged up a grappling-device which he lowered from his window, and thereby caught and pulled up the tortoise. He then replaced it by the same means with a slightly larger tortoise.

Wood repeated this operation daily, so that by the end of the week the lady was astounded by the rapid growth of her pet. Knowing that Wood was a scientist of some kind, she knocked on his door and told him about the remarkable phenomenon. Wood agreed that such tortoise behaviour was unknown to science, and suggested that she should inform the press. He maintained his daily substitutions until the newspapers were satisfactorily excited. Then he reversed the process until the lady's tortoise had resumed its original size.

In his scientific way, R.V. Jones has categorised this trick as an example of what he calls 'acclimatization by slow change'. In his book he records how the Germans played this trick in earnest during the war by increasing the intensity of their radar jamming very gradually so that it was some time before anyone realised that the radar system had become almost totally ineffective.

One hoax involving Professor Jones had the unusual distinction of literally putting itself on the map. During the war he spent weekends relaxing in Gloucestershire with his colleague Hugh Smith. The stresses and strains of war-time were relieved by such japes as the 'Bishop of Wigan' hoax in which Jones was to masquerade as the prelate on some village occasion. This was nearly detonated prematurely when one of the victims consulted *Crockford's Dictionary* and found that there was no Bishop of Wigan.

Hugh Smith quick-wittedly explained that because of Wigan's increased population – as a result of new aircraft factories – a new diocese had been formed. This news had been kept top secret so that the Germans should not be given a clue as to the importance of the area to the aircraft industry.

However, after the war, the secret Bishop emerged openly in print in Volume 39 of the proceedings of the English Place-Name Society, covering the North and West Cotswolds, where the entry for Little Washbourne includes among the list of field-names 'Bishop's Piece, named from an incident when Dr R. V. Jones, Professor of Natural Philosophy in Aberdeen, appeared there as a Bishop of Wigan'.

R.V. Jones has also told of a Joke That Never Was. This concerned Sir Francis Simon, who received a telephone call during the war informing him of an explosion in his laboratory. Naturally he refused to believe this news, since the date was 1 April. Unfortunately it was perfectly true.

As Saint Paul wrote to the Corinthians: 'When I was a child, I spake as a child, I understood as a child, I thought as a child: but when I became a man, I put away childish things.' Not everyone grows up to be so unchildish.

Readers of Evelyn Waugh's *Men At Arms* will remember, for example, the ferociously bellicose, one-eyed, monocled Brigadier Ritchie-Hook, 'the youngest company commander in the history of the Corps, the slowest to be promoted, often wounded, often decorated, recommended for the Victoria Cross, twice court-martialled for disobedience to orders in the field . . .'

In the trenches in the First World War Ritchie-Hook had once returned from no-man's land bearing as trophies not German helmets, as other daring soldiers had been known to do, but the dripping heads of German sentries in either hand. He spent the period between the wars anywhere that some fighting might be going on from County Cork to the Matto Grosso.

An insatiable appetite for physical combat was not the only childish thing the unPauline Ritchie-Hook did not put away. Not only did he speak as a child, understand as a child and think as a child. He behaved as a child. His way of showing that he was in a good mood would be to arrive in the officers' mess with a collapsible spoon which would cause the brigade major to spill soup all over his chest. On another occasion when he was in high spirits the Brigadier turned up with some trick glasses bought in a toy-shop. These he secretly distributed round the table before dinner. The effect of the glass is to cause anyone who uses it to pour its contents over his chest.

The real-life model for Ritchie-Hook was Major General Albert St Clair-Morford (1893-1945), who in the First World War was wounded four times and received a Military Cross. From 1940-41 he commanded the Royal Marines Brigade with Evelyn Waugh serving under him, thereby making it possible for him to join Captain Grimes among the Immortals. He described his recreations as 'most games'. When Waugh first met him he wrote to his wife: 'Our brigadier St Clair-Morford looks like something escaped from Sing-Sing & talks like a schoolboy from the lower fourth.'

Waugh describes 'an alarming day' when the Brigadier invited him for a social visit at the weekend. After a drive at breakneck speed in which St Clair-Morford used both sides of the road impartially, they arrived at a house which was obviously of recent construction, being built in the style known as Stockbroker's Tudor. 'Did you build the house?' Waugh asked the Brigadier. 'Build it?' St Clair-Morford snorted, 'It's four hundred years old.'

Waugh recorded that the Brigadier kept his wife in order with shouts of 'Woman, go up to my cabin and get my boots.' More peculiar was that she was the subject of constant booby traps. The Brigadier told with relish how on the previous night she had had to get up several times to look after a daughter who was ill. 'Each time she returned, he had fixed up some new horror to injure her – a string across the door, a jug of water on top of it etc. However she seemed to thrive on this treatment and was very healthy and bright with countless children.' One of them evidently being her husband.

C.O. Jones was perplexed by Ritchie-Hook/St Clair-Morford. I assumed that what he didn't like was the implied suggestion that a taste for practical jokes is childish, but this was wrong. Like most practical jokers, C.O. not only knew that he was a child at heart but also rejoiced in the fact. What worried him was that he should recognise a kindred spirit in someone as aggressive as Ritchie-Hook. Whatever else you might say about C.O., he was a man of peace, and considered that practical jokes should contribute to the gaiety of nations rather than to their mutual destruction. Certainly, practical jokes, like most humour, often contain an element of aggression, and are also often childish. Ritchie-Hook seemed to bring these two aspects too closely together for C.O.'s comfort.

COMIC CUTS

There's a well-known story of a man who went to his doctor complaining of low spirits. The doctor listened sympathetically to the patient's account of his depression, and then suggested that the man should get out more, go to entertainments for example. Why not cheer himself, by spending an evening at a performance of the great clown Grimaldi?

'I am Grimaldi,' was the reply.

It is something of a common-place that humorists and comedians are, outside their work, not only not particularly funny but that in private they often seem to verge into seriousness, solemnity and lugubriousness. In my experience this is frequently the case also with cartoonists who, like other laughter-makers, have to live with the constant fear that they will wake up the next morning to face that terrifying blank piece of paper and that nothing will happen. No matter how many times before they have done the trick, there is always the dread that next time the flint won't spark and that the paper will remain obstinately blank, without a word or a line of wit to relieve it. Furthermore, their work is of its nature solitary. Perhaps that is why when two or three of them are gathered together they tend to behave in a way that is – what shall we say? – relaxed.

An example that springs – nay, leaps, bounds – to mind

is the Cartoonists' Club of Great Britain, a group which for reasons of its own prefers to meet on licensed premises. They have in the past spent week-long holidays together, travelling the country by boat on the canals, with frequent stops at riparian public houses. This has caused much confusion in various sleepy localities where, on long winter evenings, they doubtless still recall the visit of the St Bride's League of Temperance and the quantities of alcohol consumed by its members. On other occasions members of the club have claimed to be a choir of close-harmony singers. When asked to give a rendition they have willingly obliged – all singing different songs simultaneously.

A few years ago the Cartoonists' Club spent its annual week at Butlin's Camp at Pwllheli. They were guests of Butlin's, and in return for the hospitality all they had to do was provide a daily supply of cartoons on the Camp's notice board.

A week or so before they were due to arrive at Butlin's, each cartoonist received a printed letter on Butlin's headed paper. It read:

Butlin's Camp, Pwllheli

Tel: Pwllheli 1221

Date as Postmark

Dear Guest

You may recollect that the Pwllheli camp suffered severe fire damage in 1973.

We would like to take this opportunity before your visit to reassure you that the entertainments complex has been rebuilt and that you will be able to enjoy all the wide range of facilities that Butlin's are famous for.

As well as the entertainments complex, the fire also destroyed the chalet furnishings store. We have been able to replace all items necessary for your comfort with the exception of one.

Because of the problems caused by the 3-day week
our suppliers have been unable to meet our requirements
for pillows.

We have been promised delivery during the last week of
May. However, in the circumstances we feel it would be
advisable for you to bring with you a pillow for each
member of your family.

We, of course, regret any inconvenience that this
may cause and trust that you will appreciate that it is due
to circumstances entirely beyond our control.

We thank you in advance for your co-operation in
this matter and would like to take the opportunity of
wishing you a pleasant and enjoyable stay.

Yours faithfully

N.M. Pegg
Executive Bookings

Thus it came about that some twenty cartoonists and
their families turned up at Butlin's on the appointed day
accompanied by quantities of pillows. Some of those who
arrived by rail had tied pillows to their suitcases. Car-
borne cartoonists with large families had filled the boot
with pillows, and strapped others to the roof-rack. Witnesses
of the arrival of the Cartoonists' Club of Great Britain at
Butlin's that year described the scene as 'extraordinary'.

It was not the last of the puzzling scenes that occurred
during that week at Pwllheli. It so happened that the
Cartoonists' Club had just elected Bill Tidy as their
President. Now, Bill has many outstanding qualities, but I
don't think that anyone has ever claimed that they include
having taken the Pledge. So it happened that Bill and his
colleagues were in a bar at Butlin's, expansively celebrating
his election to high office, and firing off the rounds as
though it was the Gunfight at the O.K. Corral.

Ordinary, civilian, Butlin's campers in the bar were,
therefore, mystified when they found distributed on the

tables leaflets reading:

Before you order another pint of beer, read this.
Opening the leaflet they saw a picture of Bill Tidy, in a
dog-collar and grinning madly. Against this was written:

A message from Reverend William Emanuel Tidy

This week the St. Bride's League of Temperance are
holding their annual conference here at Pwllheli.
Two hundred members and their families have travelled
from all over the country to hear their founder and
President, the Reverend William Emanuel Tidy conduct
a series of discussions and lectures on the evils of drink.
It is not a commonly known fact, but the post-1960
increase in the consumption of beer has been considerably more rapid than the upward population movement
in that period. And in 1970-71 the consumption of spirits
reached its highest level since 1921-22.

It is the aim of the Rev. Tidy and his followers to
do all in their power to reverse this headlong rush to
destruction.

But it was not until the summer of 1964 that the
Rev. Tidy first saw the light. A former dance-band
leader – some of you may know him better as Emanuel
and his Music of the Mountains – gave up a successful
and promising career to form the St. Bride's League of
Temperance.

The leaflet continued by describing how the Rev. Tidy had
abandoned his band in Uganda, returned to his home-land
'and found many friends who, like himself, had secretly
longed to give up the demon drink'.
The leaflet concluded:

Since then the League has grown in strength and
more members are attending the Conference this year
than ever before. An even wider range of lectures

has been arranged and guest speakers include Mr D. Martin from Hollywood, USA.

There may be many more people who secretly long to be able to say goodbye to drink but haven't the courage. We trust they will take heart from the success of Rev. Tidy and his faithful followers.

Naturally this caused considerable confusion among the campers, particularly as some of the members of the Temperance Movement were holding brimming glasses of alcoholic beverages and walking unsteadily, while the Rev. Tidy (who wasn't in on the joke) behaved in characteristically convivial fashion.

In the course of the week the perpetrator of the temperance leaflet hoax was identified. So was the villain who had carried out the pillow joke. His name was (let's say) Bob.

Revenge was clearly in order. What the other cartoonists did was simple but elegant. They had no wish to leave in as ridiculous a manner as they had arrived, and decided to disembarrass themselves of their pillows. Accordingly, they all wrapped up the pillows in brown paper, tied them up with string and on the final day of their holiday posted these bulky parcels to Bob's address.

In the days following Bob's return home the GPO sent several special deliveries of large soft parcels to his address. It is said that he now possesses one of the largest private collections of pillows in the world.

APRIL FOOLS

On 2 April 1698 *Dawk's News-Letter* stated that 'yesterday being the 1 April several persons were sent to the Tower to watch the annual lion-washing ceremony.' According to Roy Bolitho (in an article in the *Daily Mail*) April fooling was started by Indian princes who used to play jokes on other Indian princes on that day. He cites the case of Prince Jehawar who one April 1 massed his entire army outside the city of a rival prince. At sunrise the terrified citizens prepared for the worst. Jehawar's army charged, with swords waving, only to pass the city on either side and disappear into the distance, doubtless all shouting 'April Fool!'

It doesn't seem very likely to me. For one thing it doesn't sound terribly funny. For another the article was published on 1 April.

Equally improbable is the suggestion that the thing started with the mocking of Christ before Easter. Other suggestions include the one that it started with the Hilaria, a day of merriment in ancient Rome. Whatever its origins the idea soon caught on throughout the civilised world. In France they have the *poisson d'Avril*. In Scotland the victims are called 'gowks' meaning cuckoos. I suppose anyone who could be persuaded they had heard a cuckoo in Scotland on 1 April would be a bit of a fool. In the Lake District the victim is an April noddy; in Cornwall he's a guckaw (cuckoo again), and in Cheshire an April gawby or gobby or gob.

April fooling has long been popular among children and apprentices in various trades, particularly in printing and building. Popular fools' errands included sending an innocent lad to buy some striped paint, or a left-handed hammer, or a bubble for a spirit level, or a bucket of dry steam, or a screw-hammer, or a pot of elbow grease. Recently, however, April fooling has caught on with otherwise adult people of the kind who for the other 364 days of the year would no more contemplate cracking a joke than they would a bank. I attribute this new-found respectability more than anything else to the late, large and colossally serious Richard Dimbleby.

What he was like in private life I do not know, but his public face to the world was not one which included the slightest trace of frivolity. He was the man to commentate on grand and solemn occasions: the possessor of a voice appropriate for Westminster Abbey, and for the pomp and circumstance of great state and royal occasions. He brought to the small screen a gravitas that seemed to guarantee that, whatever the brash and vulgar Americans might be doing with the new medium, here in Britain television would maintain the sternness and seriousness that Lord Reith had established for radio. The BBC had earned a reputation for factual accuracy that had won the respect of the whole world. On the other hand it was far from famous for its sense of mischief. In those days it did not poke fun at anyone, and least of all at itself.

In addition to the massive respectability and seriousness of the BBC in general, and of Richard Dimbleby in particular, there were two other factors that made for the huge success of the Great Spaghetti Hoax of 1 April, 1957. One was that though television was just becoming a familiar object in the nation's households, it was still only on for a few hours a day, and there was only one channel. This meant not only that programmes like *Panorama* had massive audiences, but that they were discussed widely the next day.

In addition 'Abroad' was not the familiar place it is today. Currency restrictions still limited foreign travel, air fares were high and package holidays almost unknown. Furthermore British eating habits were still extremely insular. It was only a few years since food rationing had ended. There were a few Indian restaurants, but we had not yet seen the invasion of Chinese, Greek, Italian and French restaurants that are now commonplace. Avocados and aubergines were hardly known, and if presented in the shops would have been looked on with suspicion. For one thing, what were they? What did you do with them? For a generation raised on dried eggs, prunes and rice pudding, even spaghetti was an alien product coming from a far-off country of which we knew little.

Dimbleby presented the item in a wonderfully dead-pan manner. 'It isn't only in Britain that spring has taken everyone by surprise,' he began. 'Here in the Ticino on the borders of Switzerland and Italy the slopes overlooking Lake Lugano have already burst into flower, at least a fortnight earlier than usual.'

All this was done, as was the rest of the item, to a background of Mediterranean-sounding music and with film of the conventionally lyrical travelogue kind.

'But what, you may ask, has the early and welcome arrival of bees and blossom to do with food? Well, it's simply that the past winter, one of the mildest in living memory, has had its effect in other ways as well. Most important of all, it's resulted in an exceptionally heavy spaghetti crop.'

He went on to say that the end of March is an anxious time for the spaghetti farmer. A late frost could drastically reduce the crop and also impair the flavour. But this year the weather was perfect and all was well.

'Spaghetti cultivation here in Switzerland,' Dimbleby said, 'is not of course carried out on anything like the tremendous scale of the Italian industry. Many of you, I'm sure will have seen pictures of the vast spaghetti plantations in the Po Valley. For the Swiss, however, it tends to be more of a family affair. Another reason why this may be a bumper year lies in the virtual disappearance of the spaghetti weevil, the tiny creature whose depredations have caused much concern in the past.'

Dimbleby explained how the spaghetti is first picked (the film showed huge limp lumps of it being taken down from the trees and hung over the picker's arms). He went on to describe how the spaghetti is then laid out to dry in the Alpine sun. People are often surprised that spaghetti can be grown in such uniform lengths, he remarked, offering the information that this was the result of 'many years of patient endeavour by plant breeders who have succeeded in producing the perfect spaghetti.'

Then comes the harvest festival (a unique occasion, one would have thought, in March in the northern Hemisphere). The spaghetti farmers toast the new crop, drinking from vessels called 'poccolinos' (I seem to remember that there was a pseudo-Italian song of the period called 'Papa Poccolino). Finally the waiters bring in the ceremonial dish – spaghetti, of course – 'picked earlier in the day, dried in the sun and so brought fresh from garden to table at the very peak of condition. For those who love this dish there's nothing like real home-grown spaghetti.'

Dimbleby did it beautifully, and a substantial proportion of the nation was taken in. C.O. Jones was particularly fond of the spaghetti joke: witness the fact that among his effects was a much-thumbed transcript of the programme. He told me that he saw in it limitless opportunities for a medium he generally despised. How else, after all, could one hope to dupe the entire nation at one time?

It was also C.O.'s considered opinion that Richard Dimbleby had wasted a rare talent by not embarking on a career of practical joking.

An annoying feature of the daily quality press nowadays, and of *The Times* and the *Guardian* in particular is those Special Report sections on such subjects as Milton Keynes, or double-glazing, or the Sultanate of Onan. That they are boring is undisputed: the only question is whether they can actually cause brain-damage in the reader.

They usually consist of a few re-cycled articles which pull all punches in order not to frighten away the surrounding advertisements which are the purpose of the exercise. In terms of newspaper economics these supplements are doubtless necessary, but as far as the reader is concerned they are necessary evils – weary, stale, flat and profitable. Fortunately they are usually self-contained and can therefore be easily pulled out and thrown away, causing no more nuisance than additional clutter on the nation's breakfast tables and in railway compartments.

Such may have been the fate of many copies of the Guardian's 1977 seven-page supplement on San Seriffe. However, by the end of the day many a dustbin had been emptied in an attempt to retrieve it. At the Stock Exchange brokers were exchanging copies for many times the normal cover price of the *Guardian*, and today it is something of a collector's item. It was published, needless to say, on 1 April.

A front page showed the usual pictures of oil wells and palm trees by way of demonstrating that San Seriffe is a place where one can make money and also lounge about. An introduction announced that 'The ten years of independence which San Serriffe celebrates today have been a period of economic expansion and social development probably unrivalled by any other new nation.' (That's what they would say, isn't it?) This achievement had been accompanied by an attempt 'in part successful' to maintain the outward forms of parliamentary democracy. The *Guardian* proudly announced that the Special Report, edited and introduced by Geoffrey Taylor, 'attempts to recount the remarkable transformation in the life of the Republic, to inform British investors and visitors of the opportunities which have been and are being created, and not least to encourage companies trading with the Republic to call attention to their share in its development. Rapid growth brings its own problems, not all of which can be solved in total composure.' All of which is the elaborate special supplement way of identifying San Seriffe as a banana republic military dictatorship, a point confirmed by the photograph of the saluting, sun-glassed, heavily bemedalled President, General M.J. Pica.

The same page carried a brief history of San Seriffe: a small Indian Ocean archipelago whose main two islands are roughly in the shape of a semi-colon and which has had prosperity suddenly thrust upon it with the discovery of phosphates, oil and tourism. 'From a diet of mutton, goat cheese, and damson wine it is a far cry to the international cuisine offered at many of the big hotels. The thatched huts still occupied by the irrepressible Flongs, an indigenous people at the tip of the southern island, are generations away from two international airports at Bodoni, the capital, and Villa Pica. Yet something of the old tradition remains and not all that has gone was worth preserving.'

As for foreign policy, General Pica's government is firmly allied with the West, 'to which his surprisingly large air force is a source of comfort in a potentially difficult area of operation.'

A map showed the two main islands – Caissa Superiore (Upper Caisse) in the north, with its capital town of Bodoni, and the southern islands of Caissa Inferiore (Lower Caisse).

The rest of this front page was taken up with advertise-ments. One was for the post of Reader in Lunar Spectoscopy at the Perpetua University of San Seriffe. Another was for Kodak, announcing an amateur photography competition of snaps that capture the beauty of San Seriffe 'from the serene, stately grandeur of the Cap Em Opera House to the hustle and bustle of the harbour at Port Clarendon.'

Anyone who knows anything about printing would quickly have spotted that such terms as Pica, Clarendon, Perpetua, upper case and lower case, Bodoni, flong, Cap Em and so on come from typography and printing, just as they would have recognised, in San Seriffe itself, *sans serif* – the name for any type face in which the characters have no serifs (the small lines at the extremities of the main strokes of a letter). Given the date of publication you wouldn't have thought anyone could have been taken in, though it seems a number of people were. But the San Seriffe joke, which added much to the nation's hilarity, was not so much directed at its readers as at the *Guardian* itself, and other newspapers and periodicals which publish such stuff in all seriousness. It was a courageous thing for the *Guardian* to have done because it made subsequent supplements hard to read without giggling. The joke was repeated on the next April Fools' Day, perhaps not quite so successfully (hardly surprising since the element of surprise was gone) but still richly deserving an accolade which is (as far as I know) unique in the history of practical jokes. This was in reaching the Order Paper of the House of Commons. Two Labour MPs, John Ellis and Russell Kerr tabled a motion 'That this House commends the *Guardian* for the high standard of its spoof for two successive years on April Fools' Day, which in so many ways mirrors the problems and hypocrisy of the foreign policies of so-called advanced nations.'

Early in April 1973 listeners to BBC radio had the opportunity to hear an extremely learned talk about Dutch elm disease. It was given by Ronald Clothier, a man whose eminence as a scientist was complemented by a broadcasting style that had an attractively donnish idiosyncracy. It was the kind of programme that the BBC is particularly good at, making no concessions in the way of avoiding arcane technical language. Dr Clothier's voice and pronunciation suggested that he was getting on in years, and the rustling of paper with which he punctuated his talk made it clear that, though an excellent lecturer, he was not altogether accustomed to speaking into a microphone.

He started by giving the historical background. The current outbreak of Dutch elm disease (DED) was as the most severe in our history but it was not the first time that *Holandicus pernicia* had visited these islands. It has in fact occurred three times in the last 200 years, the first having been in 1780, though of course not on such a malignant scale as the current outbreak. To date, said Dr Clothier, there has been 'no actual arboreal curative to contain the outbreak.' Therefore the method advised by the Forestry Commission has been that of felling. Many farmers and countrymen have found this 'a rather draconian method'.

Dr Clothier went on to describe some remarkable discoveries about Dutch elm disease by Dr Emily Lang of the London School of Pathological and Environmental Medicine. Samples of diseased elm had been treated with a laser microscopic scanner in an attempt to isolate the diease and halt its progress. Microthermal ultrasonic waves at intense temperatures had also been used, as had viscous anoid heat-resistant alloys.

Naturally these had been carried out in a sterile chamber. This is where chance played its part. The same sterile chamber was later used for an experiment using rats in research on the common cold. The scientists were puzzled that in this case the rats showed a hitherto unknown resistance to acquiring colds. It was then found that a minuscule fragment of infected elm had been left in the sterile chamber after the previous experiment.

An eminent tree-surgeon, John Atkins, was asked to cogitate on this unusual finding. An experiment on humans was set up. Some healthy 25-year-old volunteers were divided into two groups. Both were given intravenous injections of cold or flu virus, plus liquid injections via the nasal passages (25 milligrams intravenously and 13 milligrams in the nasal cavities). Group A was left in a sterile chamber with a large log seriously infected with DED, Group B in one without the log. Group B caught colds, Group A did not.

This was clearly a major breakthrough, but there were unexpected complications. Allington, from Group A, developed a disease of the skull. His red hair turned yellow, and tests on him with the Dioxythermal scanner showed a reading of .01. Dr Clothier explained that this is on a scale so low that it is normally found only in the plant world. The implication was clear. Allington had in fact acquired Dutch elm disease.

This, said Dr Clothier, caused alarm in medical circles since it was thought 'highly unlikely that arboreal disease could be transferred to humans'. But, he concluded, there

was a glimmer of hope. Red-haired people have a very high phosphorus blood count: this, combined with a high copper trace, is the ideal humus in which Dutch elm disease prospers. Research continues, said Dr Clothier, concluding that for the time being it would be advisable for people with red hair to avoid areas affected by Dutch elm disease.

It was, of course, 1 April, and Dr Clothier was in fact Spike Milligan. Spike is one of the funniest men alive, but he does sometimes go over the top. On this occasion he was wonderfully controlled. Whether, as a result of his talk, any red-haired people were actually felled by the Forestry Commission is one of the many things neither I, nor C.O. Jones, were ever able to ascertain.

1980 was a peak year for April fooling, especially in the media. Capital Radio told its listeners that hovercraft services from Heathrow had been cancelled because of the low tide. The previous year Capital had announced details of Operation Parallax. The purpose of this was to bring Britain into line with the rest of the world by removing the 48 hours that had been lost in the 24 years since the war by switching to and fro between Greenwich Mean Time and British Summer Time. This was to be achieved by cancelling 5 April and 12 April. The announcer explained that it would be terribly inconvenient but that it had to be done. Thousands of listeners rang in with queries. One man wanted to know if he would have to pay his staff for the two missing days' work. Another listener was worried because the sale of his house was due to be completed on one of those dates. Would it still be valid? And what about people whose birthdays fell on those dates?

On the same day in 1980 the BBC's Overseas Service broadcast in Japan the announcement that Big Ben was going digital. This caused great alarm in the land of the digital watch, especially since Japan appears to be one of the few places where 1 April is a date without especial significance.

The broadcast was given authenticity with recordings of people nostalgically remembering the day Big Ben stopped, and the time it chimed thirteen instead of twelve. The BBC also offered to give the hands of Big Ben to the first listeners to get in touch.

Also on 1 April 1980 the *Daily Express* announced the unusual problems facing guardsmen at Windsor's Victoria barracks. Under the headline GET YOUR BEAR CUT! and a sub-heading featuring the typical sergeant major's parade-ground line, 'Come on, you 'orrible little man' it told how guardsmen were having to have their bearskins cut because the hair was growing too long. This sudden hirsuteness had been caused by treating the bearskins with a preparation called Otiose, a word which (any reader of the paper consulting a dictionary would have discovered) means, 'serving no useful purpose'.

On the same day passengers on a commuter train from Cambridge to London were surprised when Ministry of Agriculture officials entered a compartment and announced that as a result of an outbreak of foot-and-mouth disease their footwear would have to be fumigated. Absolutely no cause for concern. Very rarely attacked humans. Just a precaution. By the end of the journey a large assembly of shoes, boots and socks were piled up in the guard's van for the passengers to sort out on their arrival at their destination. I have half a hunch that C.O.masterminded that one.

Here are a few other things that happened on 1 April, 1980. A group called the Cads Club cemented a lavatory outside the Tate Gallery. BBC Midlands TV reported that because of the appalling weather the government had decided to cancel British Summer Time for the rest of April. Businessmen flying to Belfast from London were thoroughly disconcerted by the announcement 'In twenty minutes we will be landing in Paris'. The initial dismay of quite a few turned to disappointment when the announcement turned out not to be true.

At Simpson's store in Piccadilly window-shoppers were astonished when one of the display mannequins blinked. They were specially hired mimes.

Meanwhile the local radio station in Leicester was announcing that on account of the financial situation it was going commercial. Radio London announced the introduction of decimal time. They also reported the news that a search was on for the iceberg that sank the Titanic.

All in all it was quite a day. By comparison 1 April, 1981 passed quite quietly.

TRAVELLER'S TALES

Travellers to far-flung places have always tended to bring back far-fetched tales. An early example is *The Voyage of Sir John Mandeville*, a work which has the distinction of being the only composition of the 14th century that C.O. Jones had ever read. The reason is not far to seek. *The Voyage* is a highly entertaining account of the knight's travels in the Holy Land, Turkey, Tartary, Egypt and India, containing a wealth of information about geography and natural history, including such wonders as the fountain of youth and ant-hills made of gold dust. In fact Sir John Mandeville had no more basis is reality than the fountain and the ant-hills. The author was probably a writer called Jean d'Outremeuse, who lived in Liège at the time in question. His pioneering fake was quickly translated into several languages and for centuries continued to take in a very large number of people. Hence C.O.'s interest.

Since then there have been many imaginary or imaginative traveller's tales. *Gulliver's Travels* is an example. Others that C.O. admired were the very tall stories with which Othello won the admiration and adoration of Desdemona, with their talk of his deeds of derring-do, the dangers he had survived and the strange sights he had seen – the cannibals and 'The Anthropophagi and men whose heads do grow beneath their shoulders'.

Othello's stories were intended to win Desdemona. Other stories by people who have been to faraway places with strange-sounding names have been prompted rather by sheer mischievousness. This often takes the form of giving deliberately inaccurate information or advice to people who are about to travel into unknown territory. A few examples: Jean Cocteau span a yarn to Charlie Chaplin about having seen in China a living Buddha, a man of about fifty, who had spent his whole life floating in a jar of oil, only his head being exposed. Through these long years of marinating his body had remained embryonic and was so soft you could put your finger through it.

Bruce Lockhart tells of a leg-pull played on travellers to Africa, (especially writers). This consisted of feeding them with information about an African chief who, on seeing the sea for the first time, rushed forward to drink it in the belief that it was *crème de menthe*. This story duly found itself recorded in print as fact on more than one occasion. Likewise Norman Douglas took in Nancy Cunard with a story about a cannibal tribe on the shore of 'Lake Wyam' whose reputation for cruelty was exaggerated since 'they devour only children'. In their singing contests, he claimed, bad performers were punished by having their fingers cut off, one finger for each wrong note.

And then there's the misleading advice for visitors to Abroad. The *New Statesman* once had a competition for providing such hints for foreigners visiting London for the first time. Try out the famous echo in the British Museum Reading Room, for example.

Anyone going to places where they don't speak the lingo should be wary of the essential phrases that friends feed them. I know someone who went to Poland after being taught that the words for 'excuse me' in Polish are 'djem majtki'. This information is not strictly accurate. What the words actually mean is 'take off your knickers'. It took him some time to find out why he had such a hard time getting on buses in the rush hour.

When Jessica Mitford and her husband Esmond Romilly were about to go to the United States before the war, a friend gave them a helpful lesson about the differences in the common language that separates the English-speaking nations from one side of the Atlantic to the other. Sick people aren't vomiting in America; they're ill. Mad means angry, not insane. A nice joint consists of good pot, not roast meat. And so on. Mixed with this useful and true information was some which was rather less accurate. That a pediatrician is a corn specialist, for example. And that a mortician is a musician who plays at funerals.

But an Englishman does not have to cross the Atlantic or even the Channel for this kind of thing. Wales isn't far. They say in Wales that Welsh is the language of heaven. What they say in heaven I don't know as yet. Be that as it may, it is a heavenly melodious tongue, and it can be put to devilish purposes. For example, on a visit to the Principality, C.O. Jones picked up the phrase *Twll tyn pob Sais* and was told that it means 'God Save the Queen'. Fortunately he had no occasion to use the words since, in fact, they mean something like 'Stuff the English'. At least, that's what he was told.

On the same trip he heard of a Welshman and an Englishman who had had lunch in a restaurant in Wales. The bill had been made out, and was about to be paid when the Welshman, Laurie, asked the waitress in Welsh about the state of the roads (it was winter, and some routes were blocked by snow). She told him, and at the same time made a downward reduction in the bill. Apparently there was (doubtless illegally) one rate of pay for the Welsh and another for foreigners.

The Englishman, Bob, who hadn't understood a word, was most impressed and later asked Laurie to teach him the magic sentence which had the effect of lowering restaurant bills. Laurie obliged, and carefully coached Bob in the pronunciation of the words, '*Y mae coil clust fy nain, wedi ei daro gan fell ten.*' (I hope I've got that right.) At any rate, Bob tried it out in a number of restaurants, but without achieving the required effect. Which isn't surprising, since what it actually means is 'My grand-mother's ear-trumpet has been hit by lightning.'

Conversations with C.O. Jones on the subject of travel made it evident to me that C.O. really didn't care much for foreign climes, and even less for foreigners. Perhaps that's why he was so amused by Mark Twain's account in *Innocents Abroad* of how a party he was travelling with in Italy visited a museum where they were shown a letter by Lucrezia Borgia, 'a lady for whom I have always entertained the highest respect, on account of her rare histrionic capabilities, her opulence in solid gold goblets made of

gilded wood, her high distinction as an operatic screamer, and the facility with which she could order a sextuple funeral and get the corpses ready for it.'

Twain's deliberate confusion of the operatic Lucrezia with the historical one must have irritated the Italian guide considerably. This was, of course, his intention.

In the same library, Twain wrote, he saw 'some drawings by Michael Angelo (these Italians call him Mickel Angelo), and Leonardo da Vinci. (They spell it Vinci and pronounce it Vinchy: foreigners always spell better than they pronounce.)'

Twain found himself not at all impressed by the Italians in general and the Romans in particular. He particularly disliked the guides who were constantly pointing out yet another artistic masterpiece of great antiquity. He defended himself with a pretty devastating tactic. When shown yet another statue (by whoever it might be, even if it was an Egyptian obelisk), he would look at it with an air of complete indifference and ask in a bored tone, 'Is that by Michelangelo too?'

When he was shown a manuscript by Christopher Columbus he commented on the bad hand writing, and proceeded to berate the guide. Did he think he could mock people just because they were foreigners? We're not fools, Twain said. In America a fourteen-year-old wouldn't be allowed to get away with handwriting like that. If there were some decent examples of calligraphy then let's see them. Otherwise, forget it.

But it was written by Christopher Columbus, protested the guide. Who? Christopher Columbus? Never heard of him. The guide explained: Christopher Columbus, the man who discovered America. Twain dismissed this idea as absurd. He'd just come from America and he'd never heard of Christopher what's his name. Still, Columbus, it was quite a nice name. Was he still alive? No? What did he die of? Pox?

Such behaviour was the origin of Twain's organisation

UPJOHN, the Union of Practical Jokers and Other Humorists of North America, founded by Twain in Rome 1867. This is a secret society, membership of which is confined to North Americans. The purpose of the Union is to take the piss out of the Italians. Because it is secret it is not possible for me to detail its membership or its activities. There are those who claim that Marinetti's Futurist Manifesto was an UPJOHN work, as was the Victor Immanuel monument in Rome. Mussolini's fascist regime was definitely not an UPJOHN, however. I can't reveal my source for this information but can state with confidence that the Italians thought that one up all by themselves.

Actually there's no reason why I shouldn't reveal my source. It's the massive *Encyclopédie des Farces et Attrapes et des Mystifications* published by Pauvert in 1964. (*Attrapes* is the Frog word for hoax.) This huge tome (as far as I know the only book C.O. Jones ever possessed) was compiled by François Garadec (President-General of AFEEFA, *L'Association Francaise pour l'Etude et l'Experimentation des Farces et Attrapes)* and Noel Arnaud (Chancellor of IFFA, L'Institut Francais des Farces et Attrapes). The beginning of the book announces that these intrepid authors have further works in progress, including a dictionary of cuckolds (with telephone numbers), and a dicitionary of authors whose books have been published at their own expense. Fortunately for cuckolds and writers with more money than talent, these works do not seem ever to have appeared.

The existence of AFEEFA and IFFA and the *Institut Belge des Farces et Attrapes* shows that the French-speaking people are not short of organisations for practical jokers and hoaxers to join and there mingle with others of a similarly warped turn of mind. Apart from UPJOHN the only such English-speaking set-up I know of is the Association of Fools in Jullundun, India. C.O.'s files on the Association of Fools provide little information beyond the fact that its president, C.S. Wasan, made the wise observation that if you tell someone that there are 42,957 stars in the sky (or 3,896 or any other large number that happens to be floating around in your head) then you will be believed. But if you put up a notice saying WET PAINT on a bench, then everyone has to check the truth of this statement for themselves. (Incidentally, C.O. Jones once caused considerable confusion by putting up a notice saying DRY PAINT.)

While it's true that travel (in the sense of being there) held no attraction for C.O., journeys (getting there and the means involved) seemed to offer him a good deal of scope for practical joking. For some reason, railway trains in particular have often proved useful to practical jokers. Not long ago a railway hoax was played on the entire train-using section of the population. I am not now referring to British Rail's catering, which passed from the realm of jokes long ago, as did the time-keeping of the Sunday services which has done so much for the posthumous reputation of Mussolini.

No, I am thinking of something that happened at the time when British Rail introduced its high speed trains. This was that notices in British Rail's distinctive typographical style were posted in main line stations explaining that on account of the exceptionally high speeds attained by the new locomotives, some passengers might experience discomfort and even nausea. For their benefit vomit bags would be available on request from the guard.

An even more elaborate hoax was the Railrovers one of

September 1978. Leaflets were produced, again designed and printed in authentic British Rail style. A large number of these were printed – a few thousand at least – and were left in the ticket offices of main-line railway stations. They announced British Rail's latest cut-price offer. 'Let your Dog have its day' the leaflet generously urged. Free canine travel by rail was offered on Sunday 24 September. (Normally half the adult fare is charged.)

The wording of the leaflet was as meticulous a pastiche as were the design and typography.

Take your dog for a long run. Owning a dog has its pleasures, the companionship of a faithful friend being one. But it also has its drawbacks. Many people who do not possess a car would like to visit friends or relatives but are deterred by the cost of taking their dog or having it looked after while they are away from home.

As an introduction to its proposed 'Pet's Pass' scheme, British Rail will take your dog free on almost any train on Sunday September 24th, providing that you have a valid ticket to travel and that the dog is licensed.

All you have to do is complete the application form and exchange it at your nearest British Rail booking office or accredited travel agent for your Pet's Pass. And remember, even if you don't want to visit friends or relatives, why not take advantage of this offer and just take your dog for a walk somewhere different.

After the soft-sell came the small print, again accurately presented in authentic BR verbiage.

The freedom of choice to go where you wish!
How to book:
Complete the enclosed form and hand it in at any British Rail station, Travel Office or Travel Agent.

Condition of issue of Pet's Passes

1. A Pet's Pass is valid only if endorsed with the stamp of the issuing station/office.
2. The pass must be signed upon receipt by the person for whom it is issued. The pass is issued subject to the conditions here outlined and to the conditions, excess rules and restrictions advised at the time of issue.
3. The pass is the property of the British Railways Board and is not transferable.
4. The pass must be produced together with the ticket of the accompanying owner on each occasion of each ticket examination, otherwise the fare payable for the journey undertaken will be payable as if no pass were held.
5. The Board may refuse to issue a pass.
6. A pass will not be issued in respect of any dog weighing in excess of 35 kilos.
7. The pass is not available on certain trains on the NE coast routes, cross-channel or Irish Ferry services and sleepers.
8. In the event of a breach of these conditions, the Board may at their discretion refuse to carry or refuse to continue to carry the owner and his or her pet.

9. The person named on the pass is at all times responsible for the good behaviour of the pet whilst travelling or present on Board property.
10. The dog must be over one year old.
11. The dog must wear a collar with a disc attached displaying the name and address of the owner and the dog must at all times be kept on a lead.
12. The owner has signed an undertaking to be responsible for the good behaviour of the dog.
13. Only one pass can be issued per owner.
14. The owner must be over eighteen years of age.
15. British Rail will not be held responsible for any injury, death or accident which may occur to the dog while it is being carried or which may occur on British Railways property.

On the next page of the leaflet came a form to be filled in by the dog and its owner.

Railrover Order Form
Please read the conditions carefully.
The number of Pet's Passes for any train is limited and must be booked in advance. Complete the enclosed form and hand it in at any British Rail station, Travel Office or Travel Agent before 1600 hours on the day prior to the day of travel.
Name

Address

Name of dog

Dog licence No.

Issuing office

Destination

Return/single

I hereby undertake to be responsible for the good behaviour of the above dog and agree to comply with the conditions of issue. I am over eighteen year of age.

Signature

For office use only

I don't know which detail I like best. The 'above dog' is

certainly a nice touch, but I think the palm must go to 'For office use only'.

At the same time as distributing these leaflets the hoaxers sent out a press release purporting to come from the British Railways Board Public Relations Department to national and provincial newspapers, radio stations and news agencies. Again it was adorned with the real BR logo, type and jargon.

Release: Immediate

A recent British rail survey into passenger attitudes and habits has shown that a considerable number of pet owners who had no car would prefer to stay at home rather than incur the extra cost of taking their pet by rail.

As part of its new marketing policy, British Rail is to extend its current promotion drive to include the carriage of pets and in an experiment similar to the highly successful day out for pensioners on 10 June, it will be possible to take a dog free almost anywhere in the country by rail on Sunday 24 September.

To take advantage of the free dog pass the owner need only complete a simple application form, sign an undertaking to be responsible for the good behaviour of the dog and purchase a valid ticket to travel for himself. A dog licence will be required as proof of ownership.

The concession will be available on nearly all BR trains with the exception of certain inter-city expresses on North-East Coast routes.

Almost a third of BR's revenue is now obtained from cheap fares and special promotions. In 1977 the revenue from these areas increased by 20% to £206 million.

The scheme will be carefully monitered with a view to introducing a Pet's Pass at an annual cost of approximately £7 which can be used for all non-peak travel. Several pet food manufacturers have expressed interest in the scheme and the possibility of joint promotions utilising labels from their products is being

investigated.

In order to protect innocent members of the public the documents contained a number of auto-destructive elements, such as the telephone number on the press release which was in fact a public telephone box opposite Marylebone station. This soon unmasked the hoax, but not before it had been sent out as genuine by the Press Association, complete with photograph and a long caption, and a number of newspapers and radio stations had been taken in.

British Rail top-brass were extremely annoyed about it all and called in the Railway Police in an attempt to identify the perpetrators. The design, typography and language were all so accurate that BR were convinced that it was an inside job. It was not. And it wasn't me. But I know who it was.

What added cream to the jest was that not long afterwards British Rail made a perfectly genuine offer whereby students could simultaneously buy a rail pass and a record token. Naturally this was widely dismissed as another practical joke, which it wasn't.

The railway joke, as I've already indicated, contained elements that would protect the innocent. There are times when the innocent virtually refuse to be protected; when they cause the hoax to prosper by becoming its unwilling agents. A few years ago, a friend of C.O. Jones succeeded in hoaxing the nation – something he could hardly have achieved without assistance from those who were being duped. It happened almost by accident. He had been abroad for some months and returned during that period at the tail-end of the Heath Government which is fondly remembered as the Three-Day Week.

For some reason there had been a sugar shortage around that time. C.O.'s friend – we'll call him Jack – didn't know this. Nor did his wife, who had also been away. Wanting to make some jam, she went into a supermarket in Bristol and bought several packets of sugar. To her surprise this earned her a rebuke along the lines of, 'If it wasn't for people like you there wouldn't be a shortage.' (Since then, of course, Mrs Thatcher has made the domestic hoarding of food quite respectable, but at that time it wasn't.)

Shortly after Jack heard about his wife's experience over the sugar, he found himself in cheerful company on licensed premises. He jokingly made a remark about a salt shortage caused by a strike of Siberian miners. Obviously this was ridiculous since we don't get salt from Siberia. Anyway, salt is one thing we could never run out of, since not only does most of Cheshire consist of salt, but also we are an island surrounded by seawater.

Anyway, there happened to be someone from Taplow in the pub who, on returning to his office, repeated the story in the hearing of the tea-lady. She, dear soul, went straight out and bought a dozen packets of salt.

The story spread. A report appeared in the Reading

paper, and in no time it was impossible to buy salt in that part of Berkshire. There was soon a shortage in Bristol too and in other places. In many parts of the country, while supply remained as ever, demand went out of control for a period of some weeks during which salt became widely unavailable. Even given the somewhat hysterical mood of the time, it is remarkable that such a simple and unplanned hoax could have taken in so many for so long. C.O. was vastly encouraged by the whole thing. It seemed clear to him that with so many willing if unwitting participants, a practical joke, if its constituents were carefully tailored, could involve not a single country, but continents, hemispheres – the world!

'What's become of Waring since he gave us all the slip?' Thus, if I remember rightly, Robert Browning began a poem about an acquaintance he and his mutual friends had lost touch with. The same question could be asked about C.O. Jones. What *has* become of him? Frankly, I don't know, although it is a subject I often discuss with other of his friends and past victims (which usually came to the same thing). I know someone who is convinced that he is Sir Keith Joseph's script-writer. Another believes equally strongly that C.O. actually *is* Sir Keith Joseph. Yet another sees the hand of C.O. behind the economic policy of the Thatcher government.

And then there are those who say that C.O. is no more. That he has gone to meet the Great Practical Joker in the sky. I don't believe this. It's not just that I am reluctant to think that my old friend (yes, I think I can use that word, in spite of everything) has shuffled off this mortal coil. It's rather that I can't think who the hell else, during the great salt shortage, would have sent me a packet of Cerebos salt with a fiver attached to it. And who it is that from time to time upsets the domestic harmony which normally reigns in my household by sending through the post things which require so much explaining away. Like the box of chocolates which the postman delivered as a gift from Mlle Frou-Frou La Touche, Personal Services Ltd. Or the heavily-scented frilly female underwear accompanied by a note reading 'A memento from Muffkins'. Or – but I won't go on. The question is – will he?